Violin

The Magic of Music Theory

Pre-Reading B

Kristin Campbell

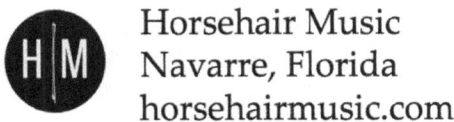

Horsehair Music
Navarre, Florida
horsehairmusic.com

Pre-Reading B Violin ISBN 978-1-959514-09-1; Library of Congress Number: 2024909186
Pre-Reading B Viola ISBN 978-1-959514-10-7; Library of Congress Number: 2024909198
Pre-Reading B Cello ISBN 978-1-959514-11-4; Library of Congress Number: 2024909201

This book is dedicated to Laura Crawford and Charles Regauer, directors of the Centenary Suzuki School in Shreveport, Louisiana. Thank you for welcoming me into your Suzuki family and giving me a platform to teach theory to string students.

Special thanks to Ruth Coleman for her editorial help. Thanks to all the students who have tested out these pages and activities.

Graphics:
Cover Design: Christiana Hudson and Kristin Campbell
Hand image by www.vectorportal.com
String instrument, fingerboard and bow images by Kristin Campbell
Haydn Graphic Licensed from Florida Center for Instructional Technology
All other images from www.freesvg.com

To the student:

Welcome to the Magic of Music Theory! Did you know that when you write things on paper it helps you remember them? This book is to help you remember things that you have learned in your lesson about your violin. This book will help you learn how to read and write music. Your practice partner will help you to read and do each lesson. If you have any questions, be sure to ask your teacher. When you finish this book, you will know and understand more about your violin and playing music. It's like magic, the magic of music theory!

To the practice partner:

You are the violin hero. Practicing isn't always fun, and it's not always easy. But in this journey of learning to play the violin, you get to walk alongside a child and give them the gift of music that will last for a lifetime.

My hope with this series is that it creates happy memories as you work through the book together. Playing games, reading stories, coloring, listening to music, learning how to draw and write music. Depending on age and reading ability, you may need to read the pages to the student. You can learn along with them. Don't be afraid to help and lead the student to the answer. These might new concepts and your child may not grasp it the first time it is introduced. That's ok! You will find a lot of review built in through out the book and they will begin to understand and remember. This is the process of learning.

Keep theory time short! You can choose to do the lesson at the end of one practice session, or you could choose to divide it up with just a little bit each day. It's up to you. Ask your teacher if they would like to do the "What Do You Hear?" pages in the lesson. You can also access videos online or download free mp3 tracks with each question played by a violinist. The answers for each question are given on the video/ track, so that the student gets immediate feedback in the learning process. I hope you enjoy the magic of learning music theory

To the teacher:

I created this series because I realized that my students needed some basic skills before starting note reading. I needed something they could do at home and not give up valuable lesson time that would teach and review these concepts. By writing and drawing, I wanted to engage a different part of their thinking in the music learning process. This pre-reading series teaches students recognize, draw music notation, symbols, reading up and down on the page and all while relating it to the fingerboard. You can use this for students who are already reading music to reinforce concepts. Or you can use it with students who are getting ready to begin note reading to introduce these concepts.

The aural skills pages, "What Do You Hear?" can be done in the lesson or through online videos or free mp3 tracks. (Visit www.horsehairmusic.com to download the mp3 tracks.) Suggested recordings are linked to online videos to listen to while doing the coloring pages, but feel free to select your favorite artist or recording to share with your student.

The Magic of Music Theory Series Guide

Use this chart to help find the level that is right for your student.

Ages 4-6 Early Book 1	Ages 4-6 Mid Book 1	Ages 6-7 Late Book 1	Ages 6-8 Book 2
Pre-Reading A	**Pre-Reading B**	**Primer**	**Book 1**
• Student has been playing the violin for a couple months and has learned Twinkle, Twinkle Little Star • Parent guides the student through the workbook. • Student can write English alphabet letters. • Student is not ready to read staff notation. • After completion move to Pre-Reading B.	• Student has completed Pre-Reading A. • Student knows A & E string fingerboard notes. • Student recognizes basic rhythm symbols. • Parent guides the student through the workbook. • Student can write the English alphabet letters. • After completion student will be ready to begin learning staff notes. • After completion move to Primer.	• Student is reading books at GRL level A–D. • Student is ready or has begun note reading. • Student can draw all letters of alphabet. • Primer level covers all the concepts in Pre-Reading A and B, and introduces staff notes for 2 upper strings. • After completion move to Book 1.	• Student is reading books at GRL level D–H. • Student is reading staff notes for upper 2 strings. • Book 1 covers all the concepts in Pre-Reading books and Primer and introduces staff notes for D and G strings. • After completion move to Book 2.

Table of Contents

Lesson 1

1. Draw a line matching the name with the part of the violin or bow.

pegs   neck   E string   A string   front

f holes   fine tuners   fingerboard

scroll   ribs   D string   G string   nut

bridge   chin rest   button

grip   frog   screw

stick   wrapping   tip   horsehair

2. In each rain drop write one letter of the music alphabet in order.

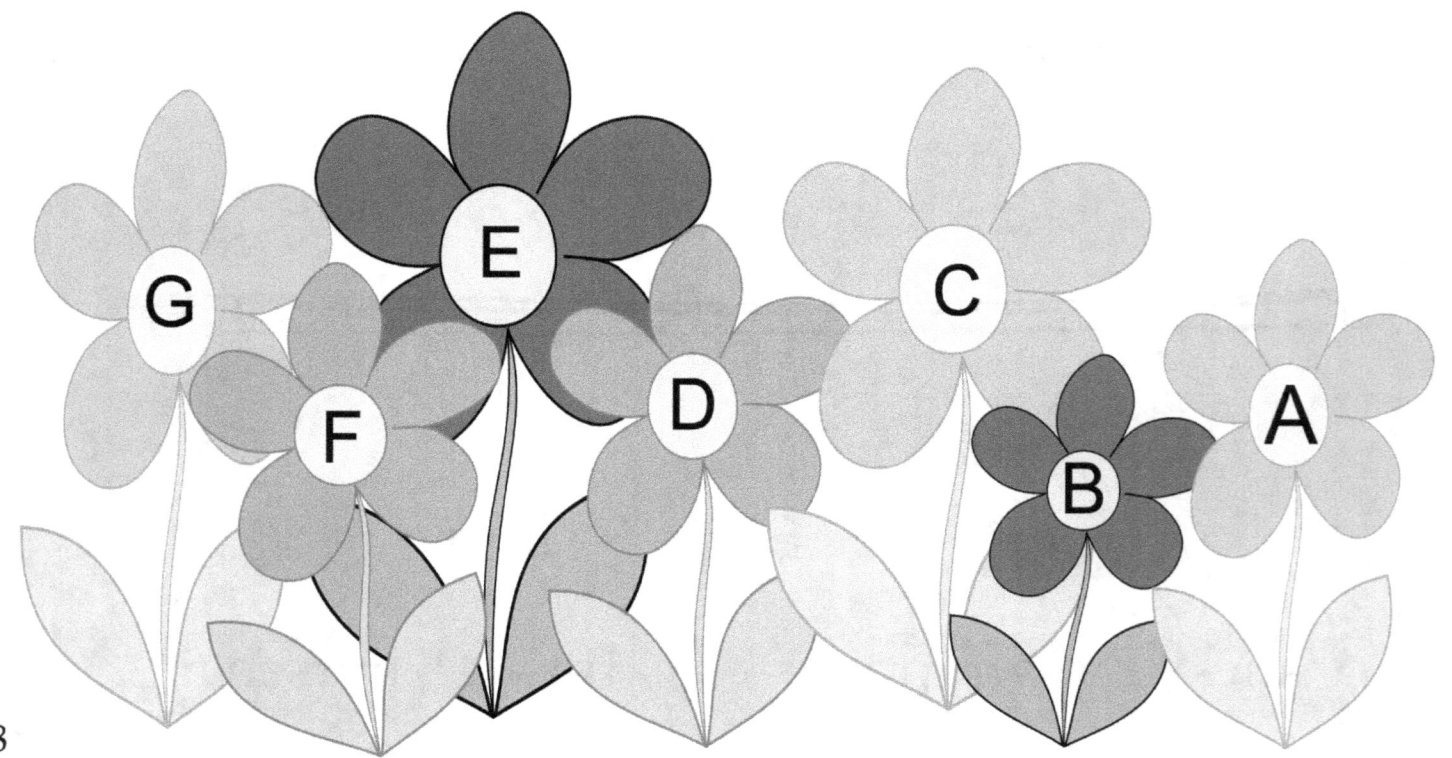

3. Say the music alphabet BACKWARDS! Say each letter as your practice partner points to each flower.

The Magic of Music Theory Pre-Reading B - © 2024 Horsehair Music. Photocopying prohibited.

Lesson 2

1. Write in letter names in each house. Write the finger numbers in the circles.

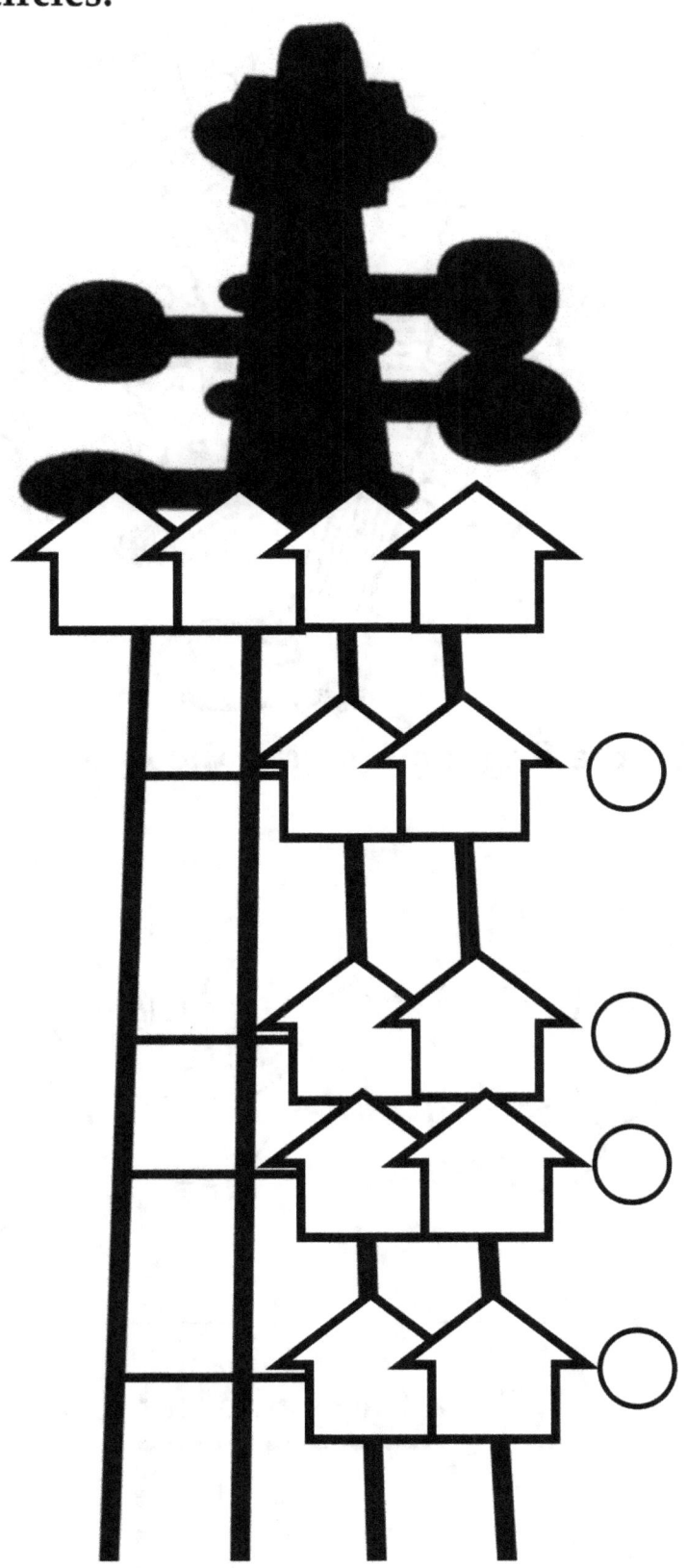

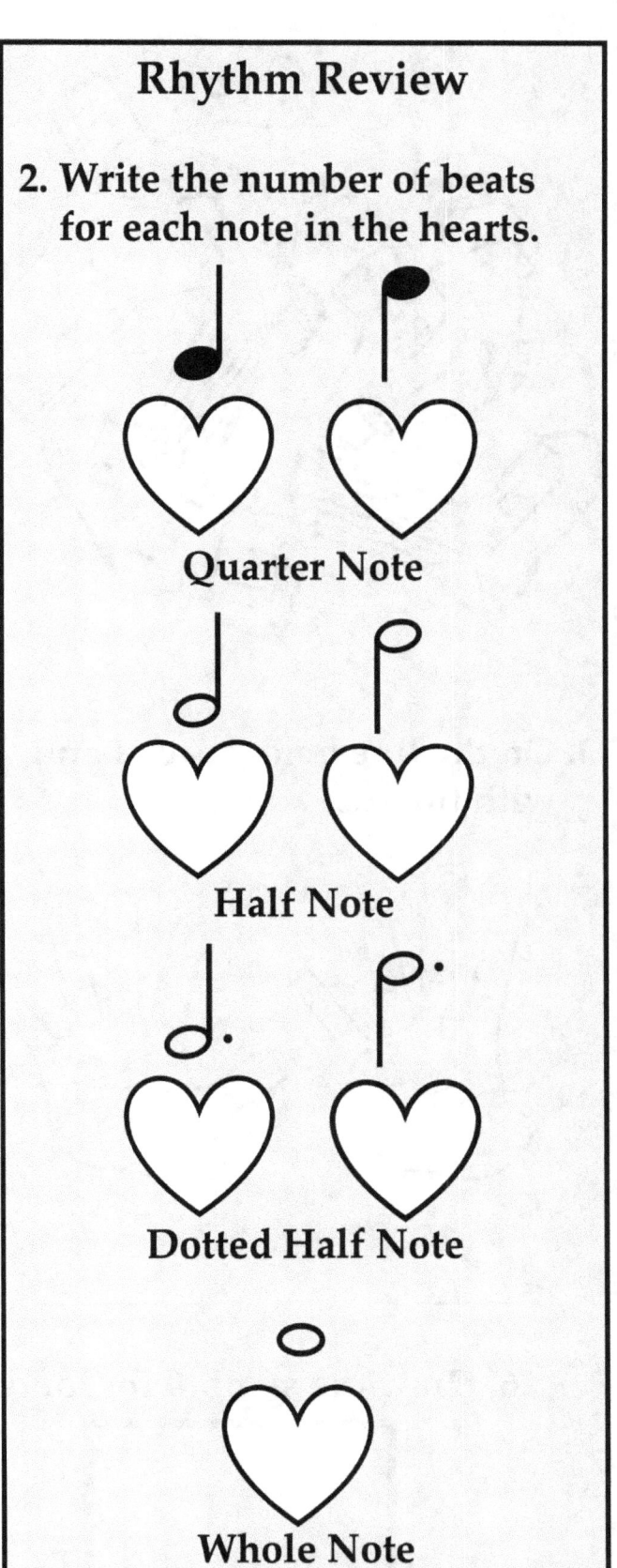

3. Your practice partner will place a coin on a house. On your violin play Mississippi Stop Stop on the covered note.

4. The socks got mixed up! Draw a line to pair the socks with the notes on the socks to the number of beats.

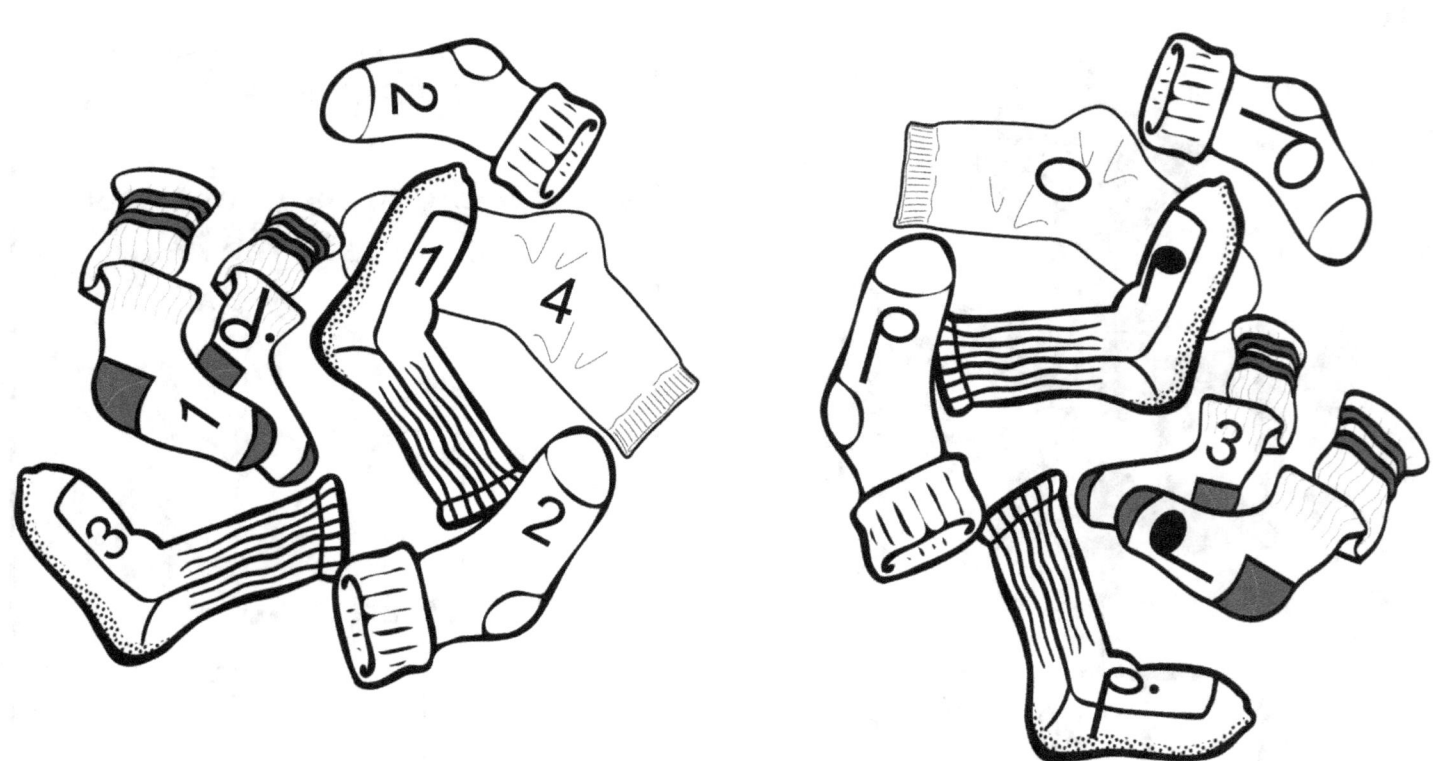

5. On the line below each hand, write the finger number of the finger with the star.

_____   _____   _____   _____

6. Draw the symbol for loud.

7. Draw the symbol for soft.

Lesson 3

1. Write one letter of the music alphabet in each blank beginning on D.

D __ __ __ __ __ __ __

Each finger on the left hand has a house on the D string. The letters on the D string are the same as some letters on the A and E string. But the letters on the D string sound **lower.** Notice that the 3rd finger is just G, *not* G-sharp!

The house at the beginning is **Open D.**

① 1st finger's house on D string is called **E.**

② 2nd finger's house on D string is called **F#.** (F-sharp)

③ 3rd finger's house on D string is called **G.**

④ 4th finger's house on D string is called **A.**

2. Write the letter in each D string house.

3. Write the letter in each D string house.

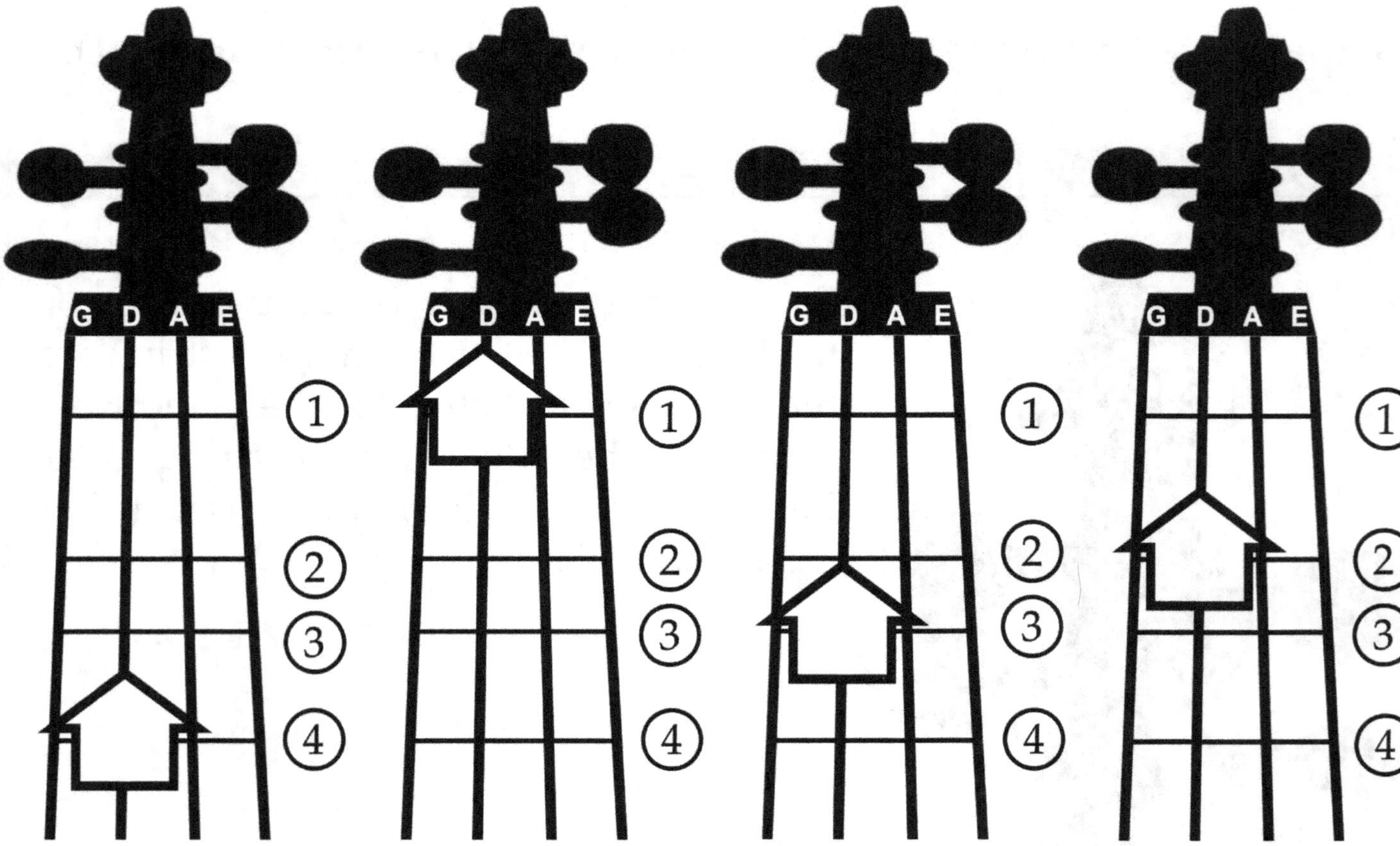

4. Help Farmer Fred label the haystacks by circling the string you hear.

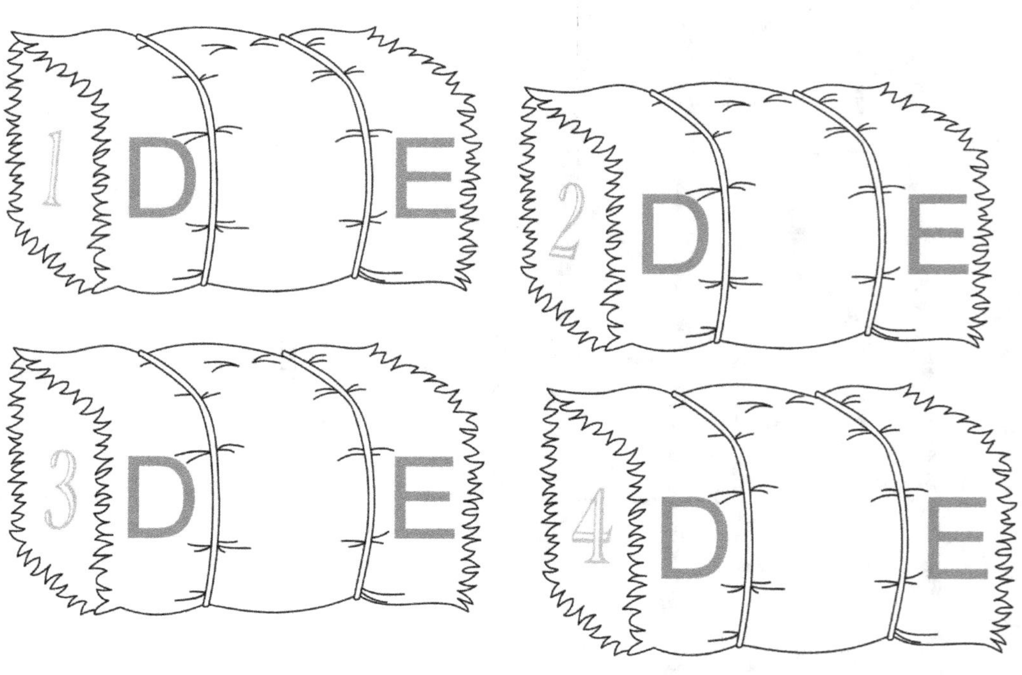

1 D   E
2 D   E
3 D   E
4 D   E

The teacher may choose from these examples:

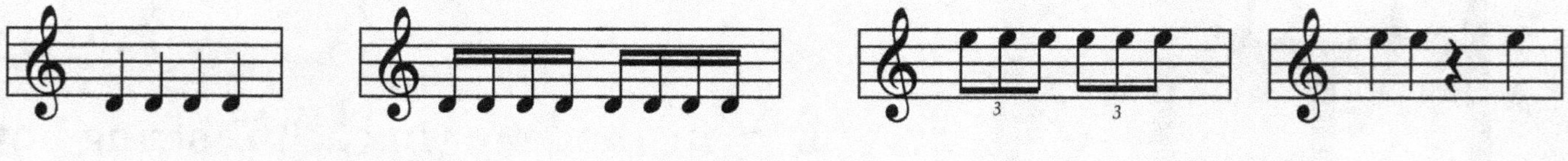

The Magic of Music Theory Pre-Reading B - © 2024 Horsehair Music. Photocopying prohibited.

Lesson 4

Write the letter in the scoop that lives on either side of the letter in the middle scoop. Start at the bottom scoop and go up through the alphabet.

What do you hear? #1

Help Busy Bee know which cell to put the nectar in. Circle the letter name of the string that you hear.

1 D A E

2 D A E

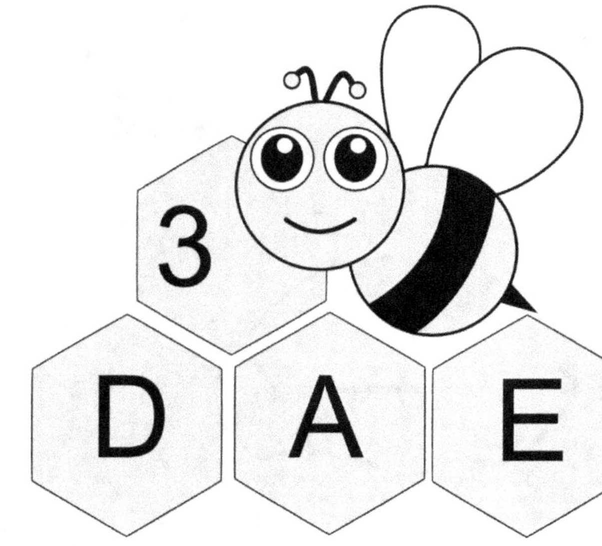

3 D A E

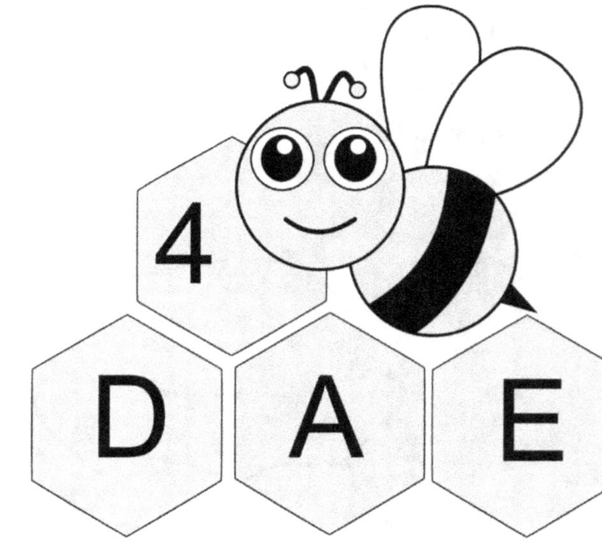

4 D A E

The Magic of Music Theory Pre-Reading B - © 2024 Horsehair Music. Photocopying prohibited.

The teacher may choose from these examples:

LaDee Bug

G E A D

F# G

A E

E

D F#

F# A

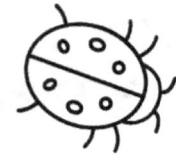

LaDee Bug

D String Game

2 Players

What you need:
 5 pennies
 5 dimes
 1 die
 2 cups

How to play:

1. Each player chooses the type of coin they wants to use, pennies or dimes.
2. Place your coins in a pile or cup near the game board.
3. Take turns rolling the die. The number on the die is a finger number. Place a coin on the spot that matches the D string letter for the finger number rolled.
4. The first player to place all their coins on the ladybug wins.
5. If you roll and there is no letter that matches that finger, the next player takes a turn.

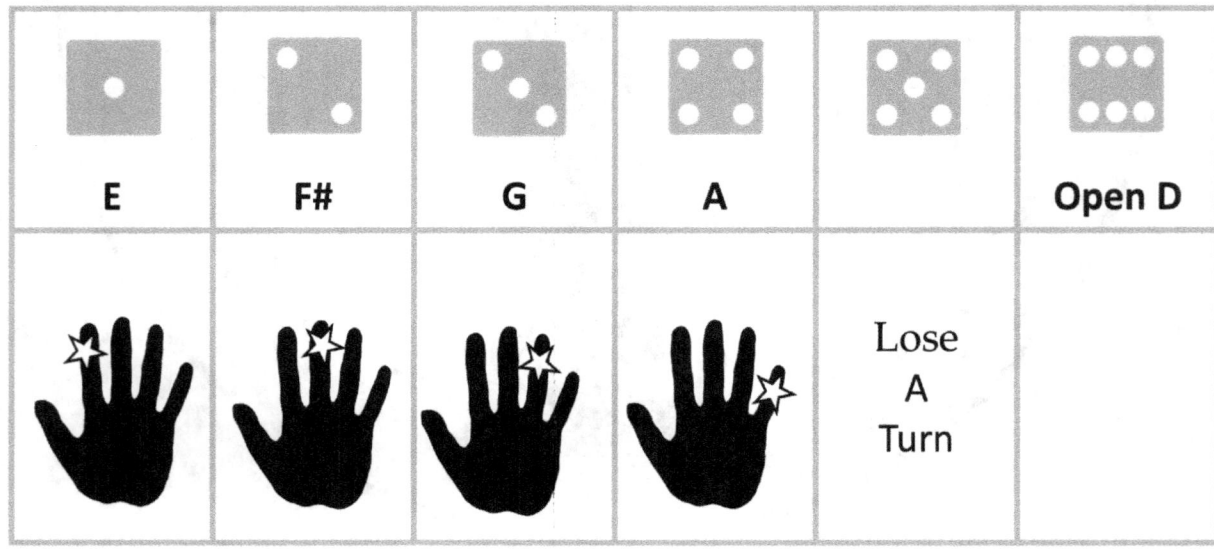

Lesson 5

In music we have to say the music alphabet forwards and backwards. When the notes get higher, we go forward in the music alphabet. When the notes go lower, we go backwards in the music alphabet.

1. Starting with the first book and going forward, write one letter of the music alphabet in each book.

2. Starting with the last book and going backwards, write one letter of the music alphabet in each book.

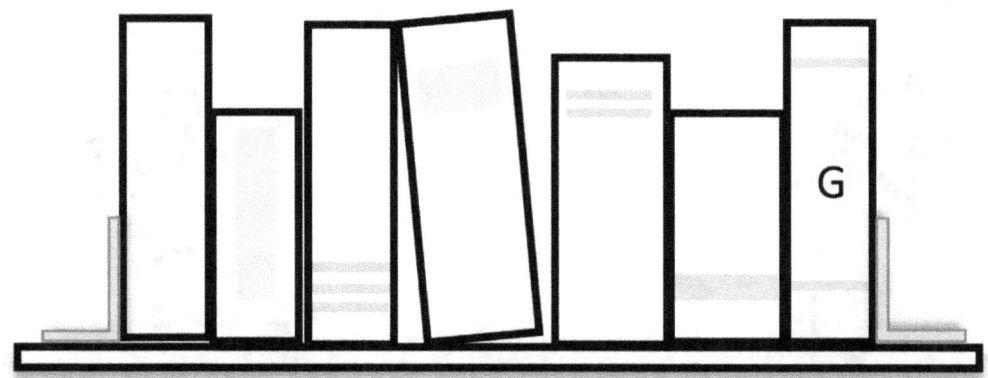

3. Draw a line from the term to the part of the note.

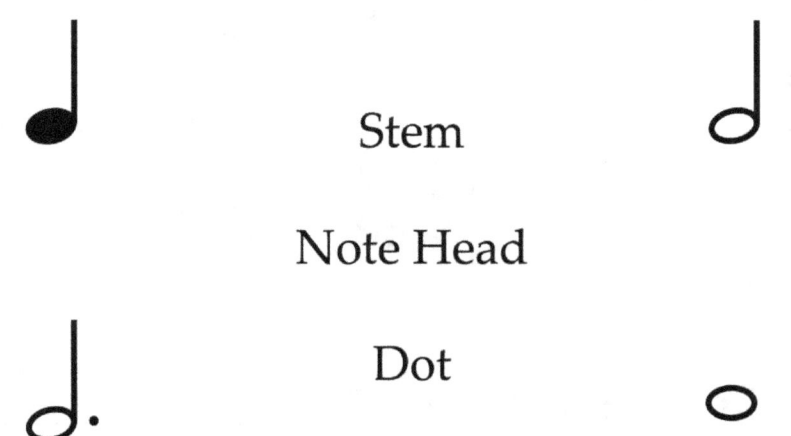

Stem

Note Head

Dot

Lucy can't remember where she put her rosin. So, she asked Sherlock Tones to help her find it. Sherlock Tones traced Lucy's steps backwards through the music alphabet.

4. To help Sherlock Tones, write one letter of the music alphabet going backwards in each shoe print.

6. Where did Sherlock Tones find the rosin? _____

Lesson 6

Listen as your teacher plays notes stepping up on the A string.

Listen as your teacher plays notes stepping down on the A string.

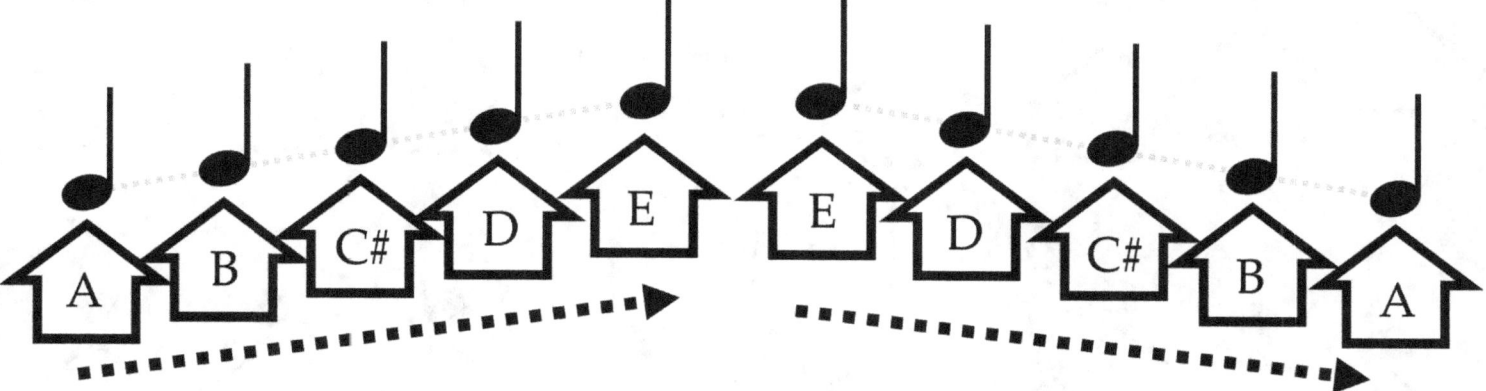

A repeated note is when we play the same note.

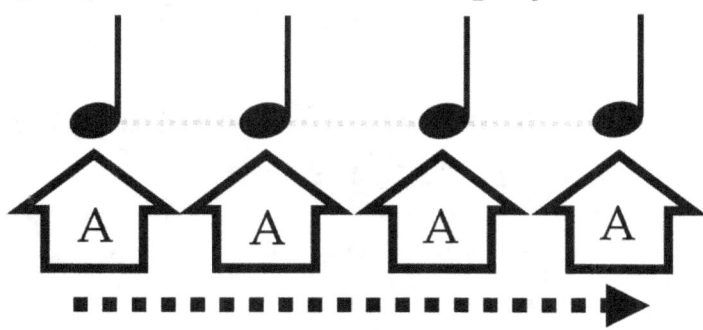

1. Fill in the A string letters stepping up and stepping down.

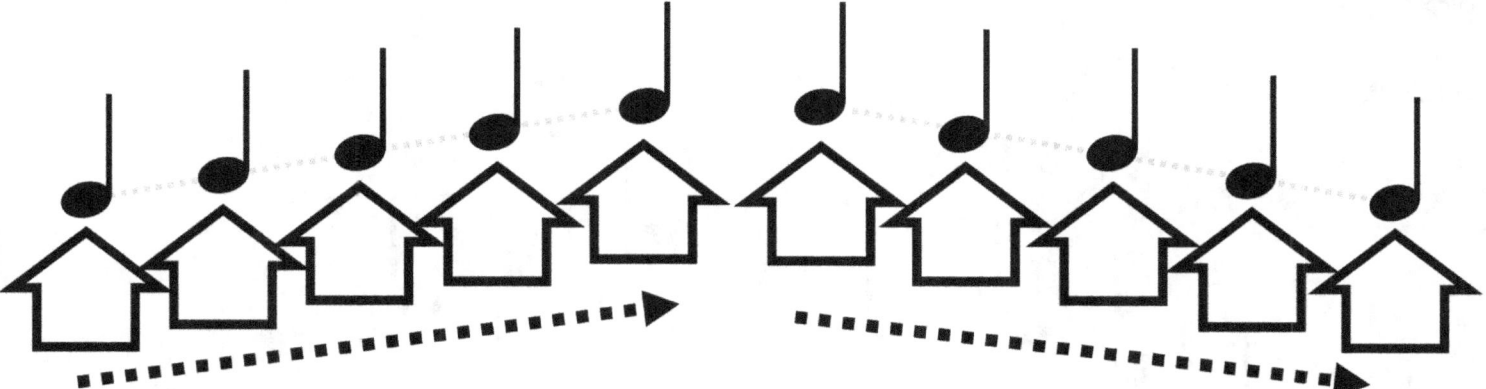

2. Fill in the D string letters stepping up and stepping down

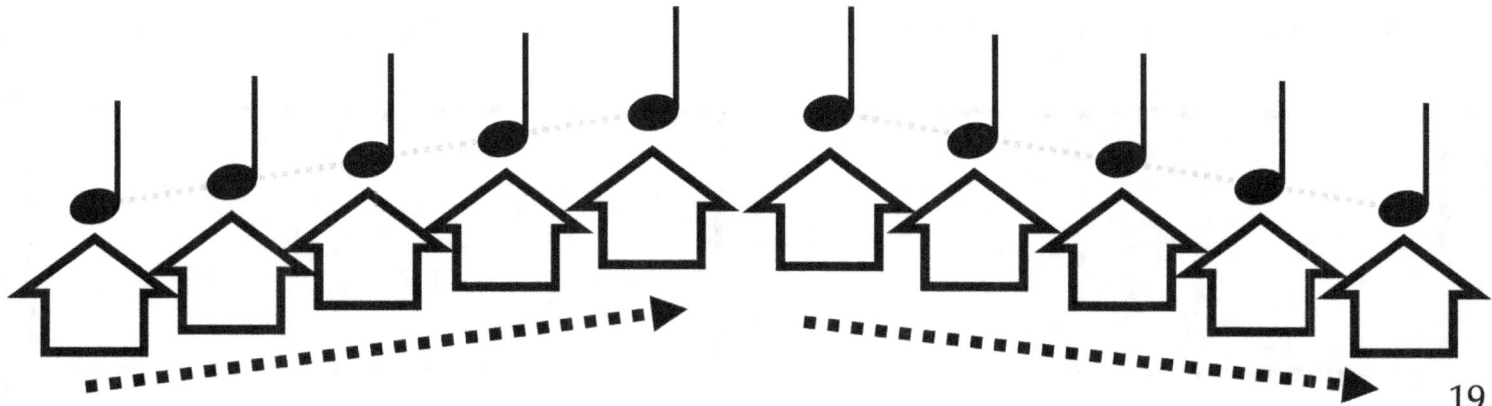

3. Follow the direction of the quarter notes to fill in the house letters.

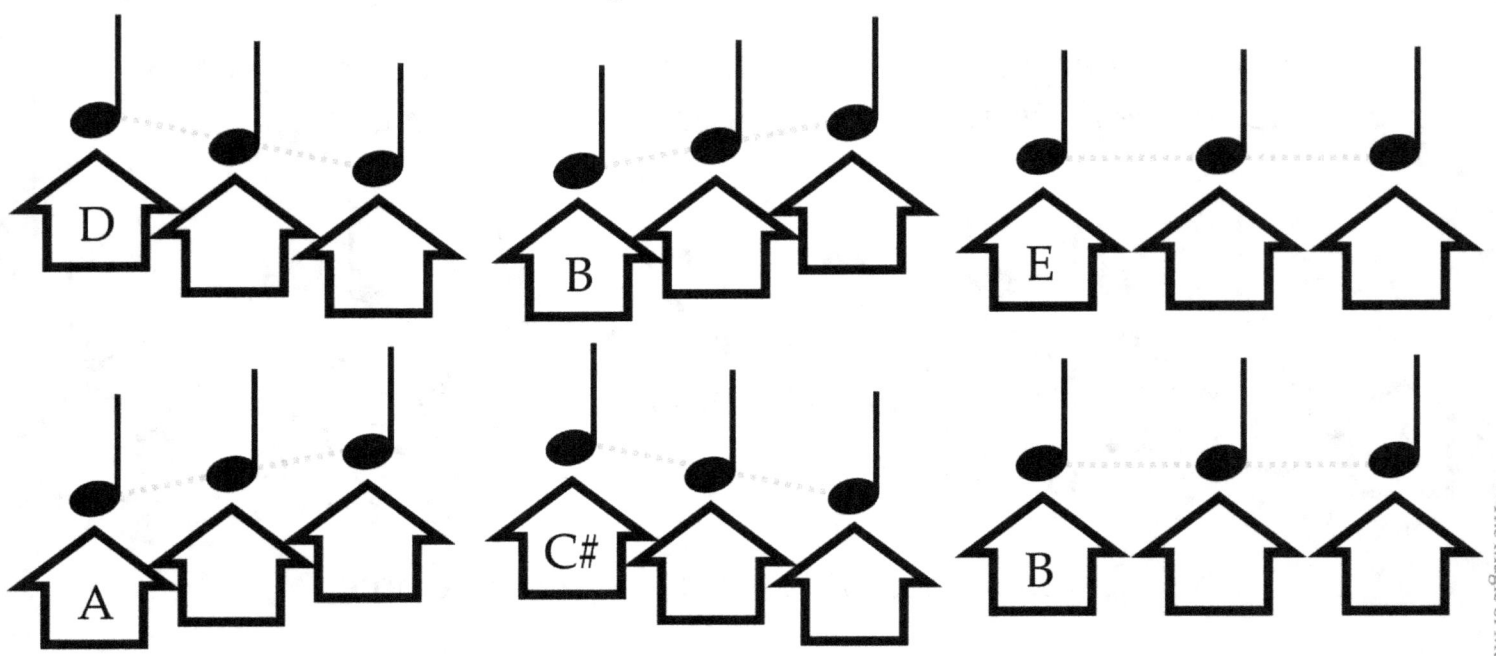

4. Pirate penguin lost his way to his igloo. Follow the quarter note map directions and write the letter in each ice cube.

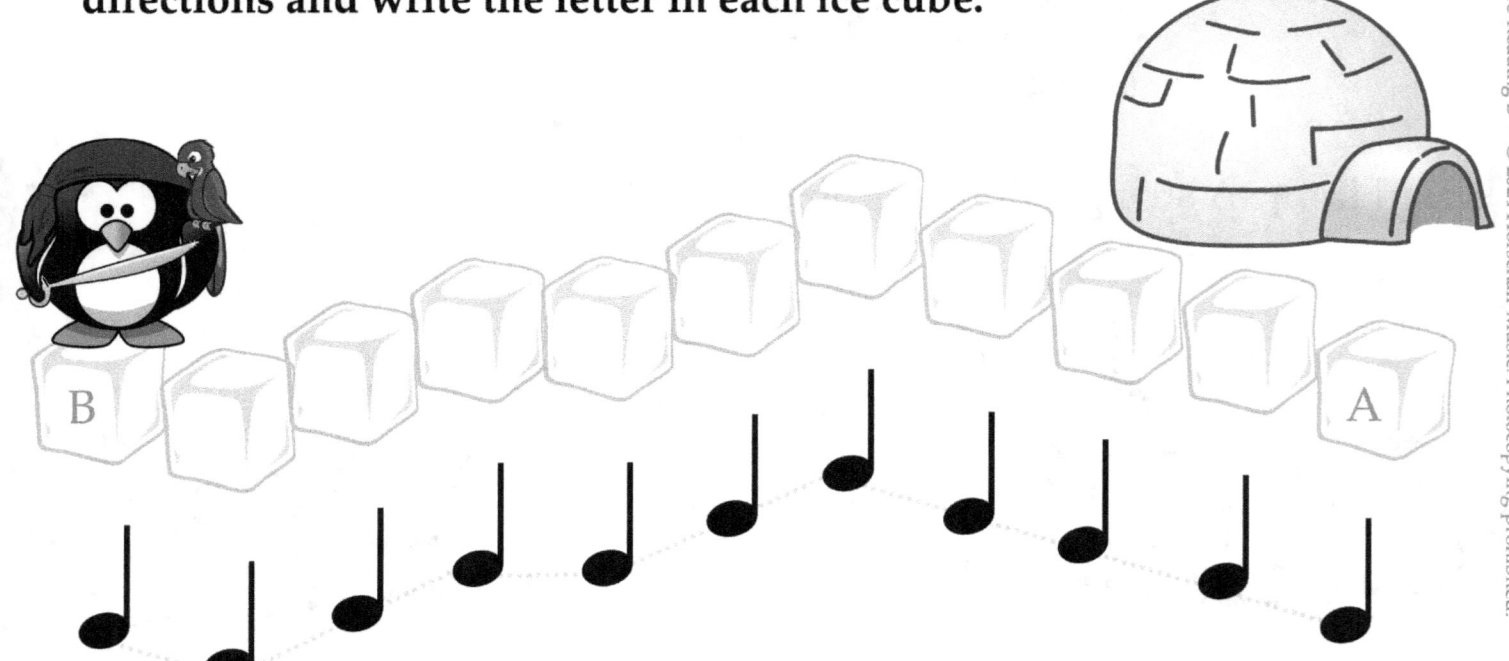

5. Draw 3 quarter notes stepping up.

6. Draw 3 quarter notes stepping down.

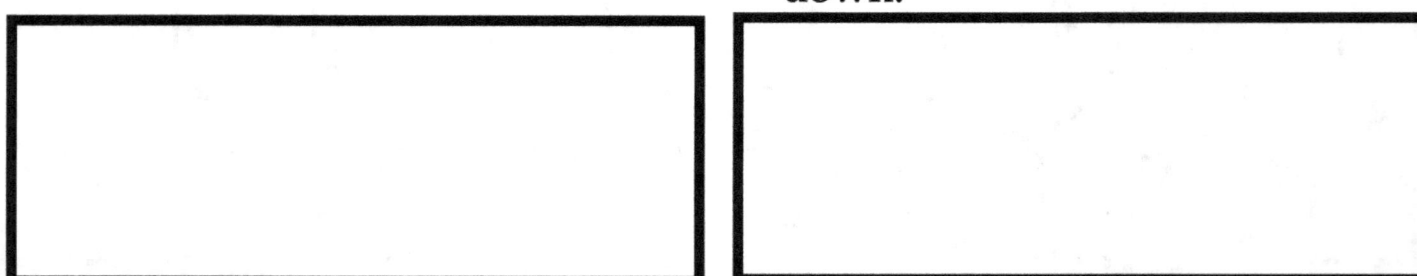

The Magic of Music Theory Pre-Reading B - © 2024 Horsehair Music. Photocopying prohibited.

What do you hear? #2

Place a coin in each circle. If the notes you hear go up, push a coin up onto the plane taking off. If the notes you hear go down, push a coin down to the plane landing.

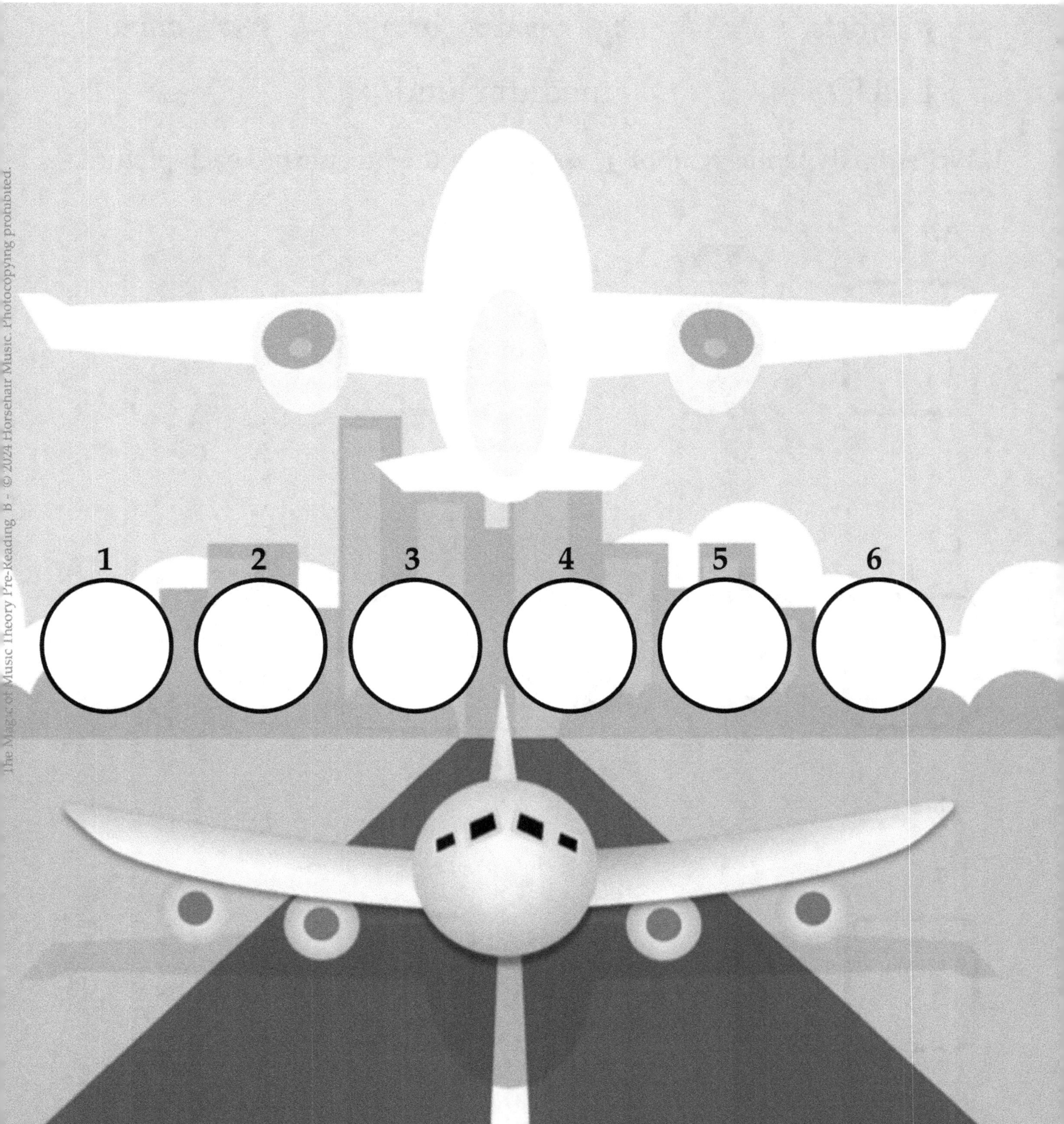

1 2 3 4 5 6

* For extra practice at identifying up and down, see page 78.

21

Lesson 7

Dynamics tell us how loud or soft to play. **Forte** [four-tay] means loud and **piano** means soft. In the middle is **mezzo forte**. Mezzo is pronounced: met-zoh. In Italian two z's make a soft sizzling sound. Mezzo forte means medium loud.

f = *forte*　　　　　*mf* = *mezzo forte*　　　　　*p* = *piano*

LOUD　　　　　　　medium loud　　　　　　　soft

1. Write the dynamic symbol *f*, *mf*, or *p* in the box next to each picture.

A.

B.

C.

D.

E.

F.

Circle f if you hear forte. Circle mf if you hear mezzo forte. Circle p if you hear piano.

1.

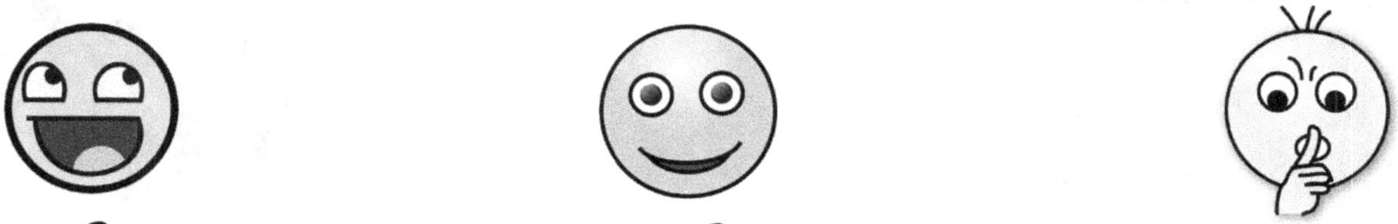

f mf p

2.

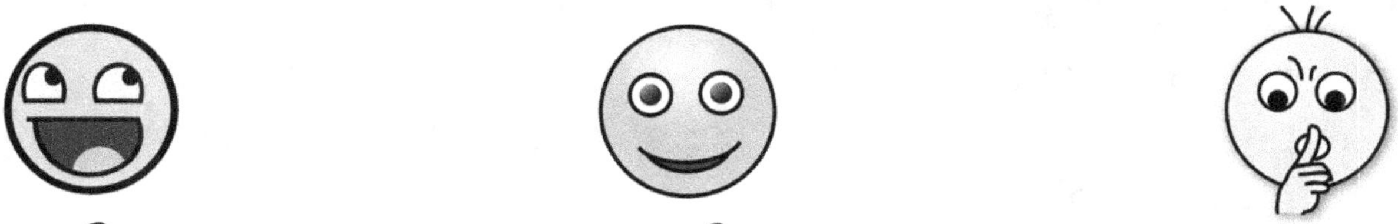

f mf p

3.

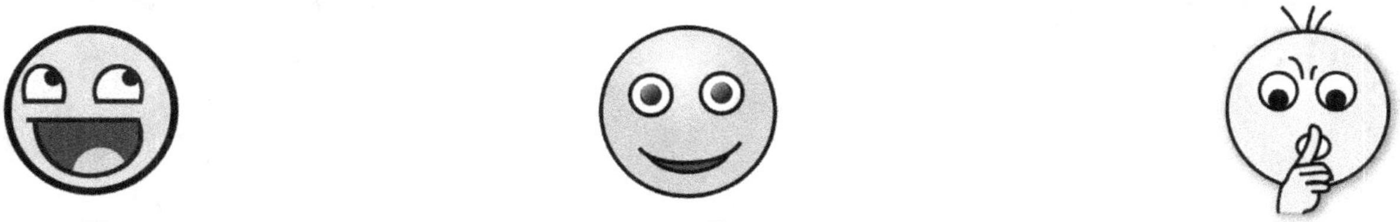

f mf p

4.

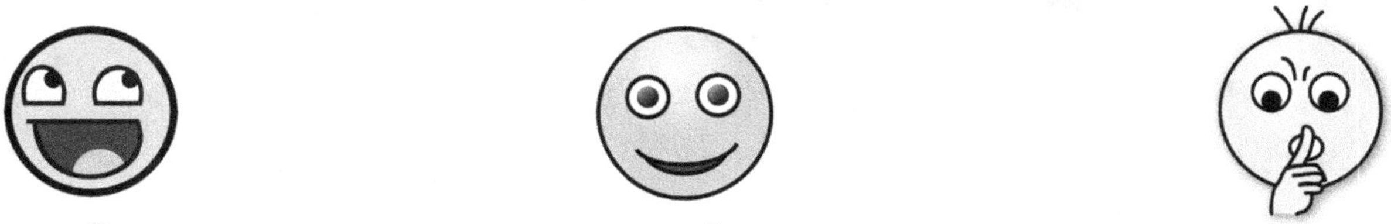

f mf p

* For extra practice at identifying dynamics, see page 79.

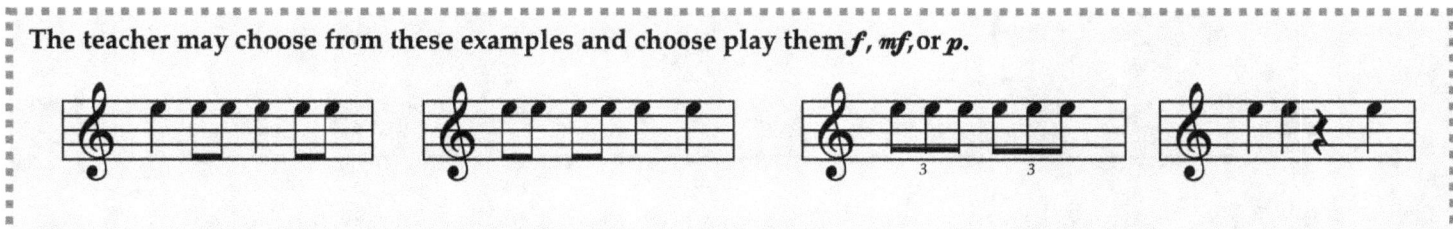

The teacher may choose from these examples and choose play them f, mf, or p.

Lesson 8

A **composer** is a person who writes music. Anybody can be a composer. Wolfgang Amadeus Mozart [Mote-zart] is composer who lived over 200 years ago. Mozart began composing when he was just 6 years old. So, guess what? Even kids can be composers!

Compose a song on the D string.

1. The first and last note is written for you.
2. Pick 7 notes on the D string and write the letters on each line.
3. Write a dynamic for your song in the circle.
4. Think of a title for your song.
5. Make up words to go with your song. Your practice partner can write words under each letter for you.
6. Play your piece!

My Song Name:

_____

D   _____   _____   _____

Dynamic: ◯

_____   _____   _____   _____ D

The Magic of Music Theory Pre-Reading B - © 2024 Horsehair Music. Photocopying prohibited.

A **string quartet** has 4 stringed instruments - 2 violins, 1 viola and 1 cello. One of Mozart's teachers, Franz Joseph Haydn [High-den] composed 83 string quartets. He is known as the "father of the string quartet." Haydn loved a good joke. Once, he wrote long sections of extremely soft music. Then, he added an extra loud chord just to see if he could make the audience jump in surprise. He called the piece "The Surprise Symphony."

What's the difference between a violin and a fish?

You can't tuna fish

1. **Listen to Haydn's String Quartet in E-Flat major, Opus 33 No. 2, IV. Finale, "The Joke." While you listen color the instruments in a string quartet. Did you hear Haydn's musical joke?**

Second Violin

Viola

First Violin

Cello

Lesson 9

1. Write one letter of the music alphabet in each blank beginning on D.

<u>G</u> ____ ____ ____ ____ ____ ____ ____

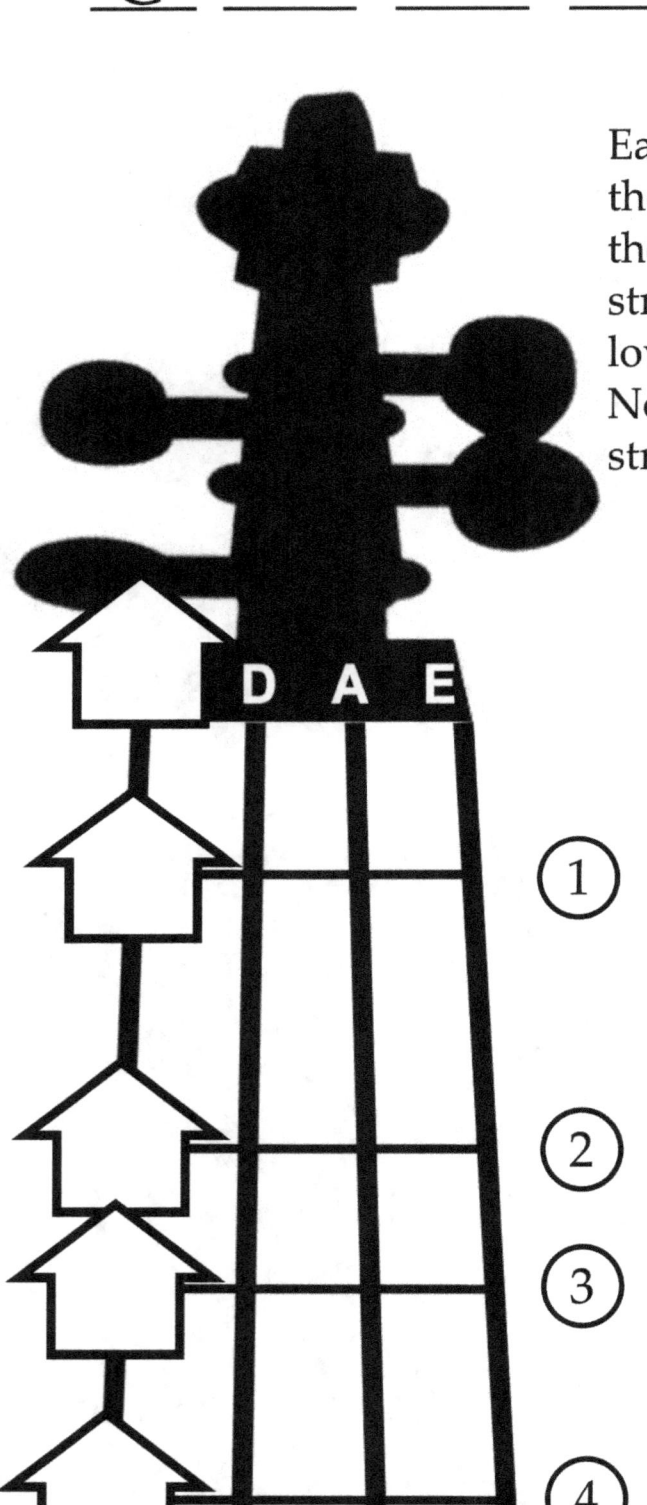

D A E

Each finger on the left hand has a house on the G string. The letters on the G string are the same as some letters on the other three strings. But the pitches on the G string sound lower than the pitches on the other strings. Notice that none of the fingers on the G string have sharp in their name!

The house at the beginning is **Open G.**

① 1st finger's house on G string is called **A.**

② 2nd finger's house on G string is called **B.**

③ 3rd finger's house on G string is called **C.**

④ 4th finger's house on G string is called **D.**

2. Write the letter in each G string house.

3. Write the letter in each G string house.

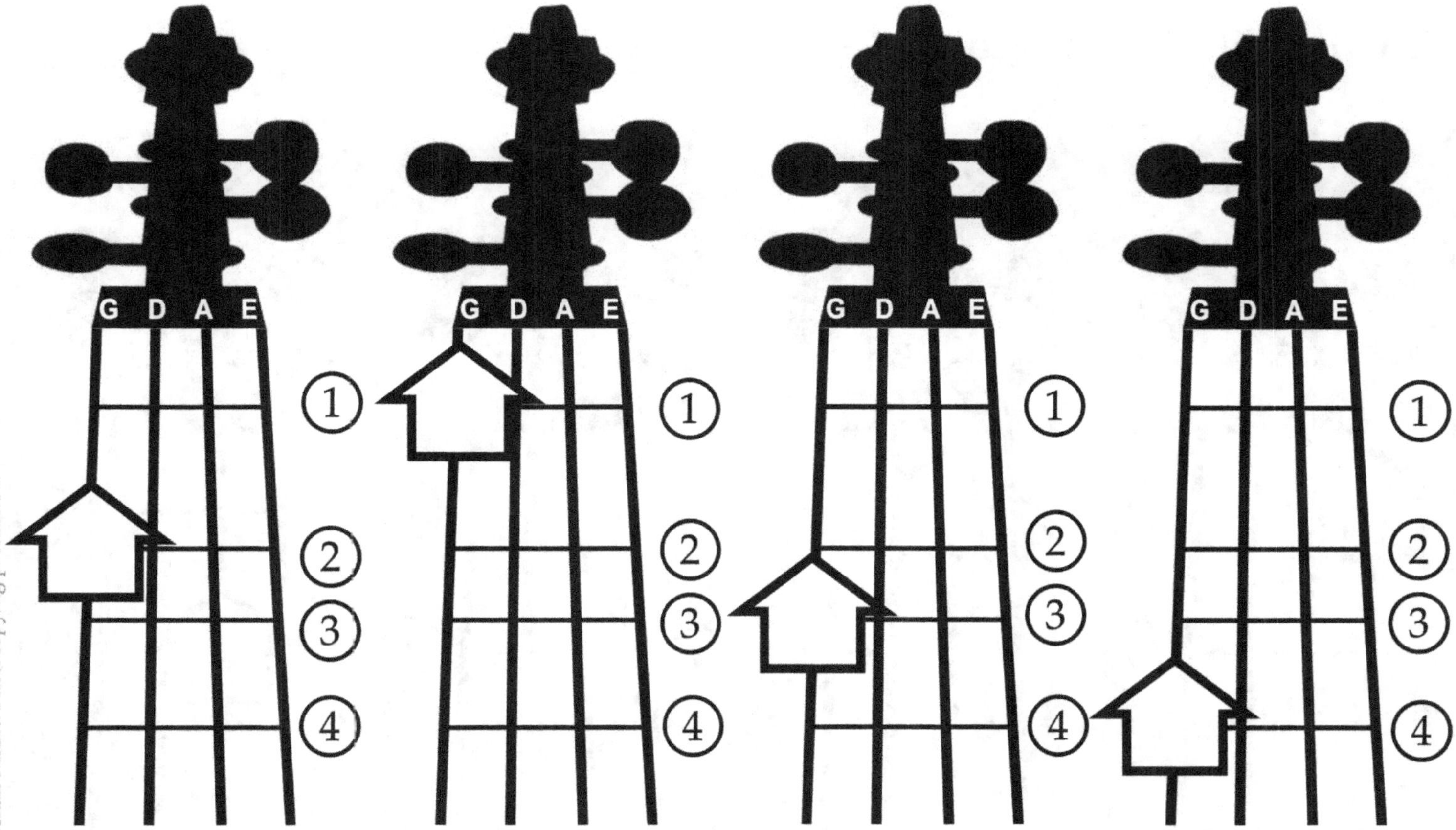

G D A E   G D A E   G D A E   G D A E

① ② ③ ④ (repeated for each fingerboard)

4. Write the finger numbers on each finger.

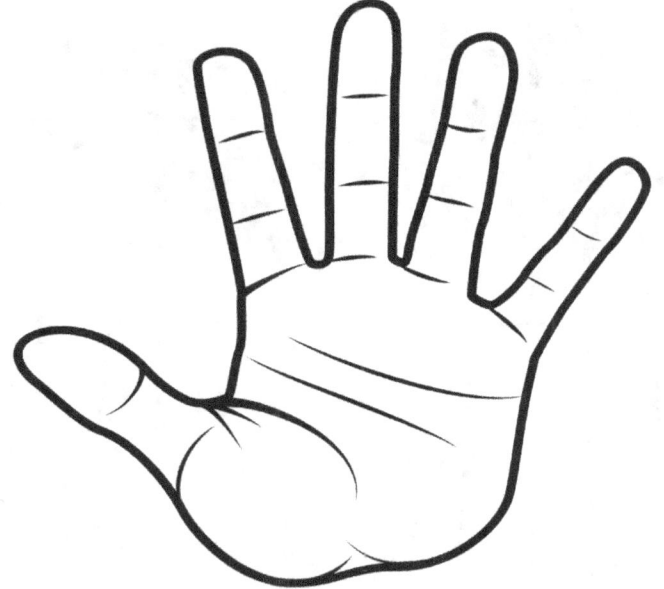

5. What finger plays A on the G string?

_____

6. What finger plays B on the G string?

_____

7. What finger plays C on the G string?

_____

8. What finger plays D on the G string?

_____

Lesson 10

1. Write the letter in each house.

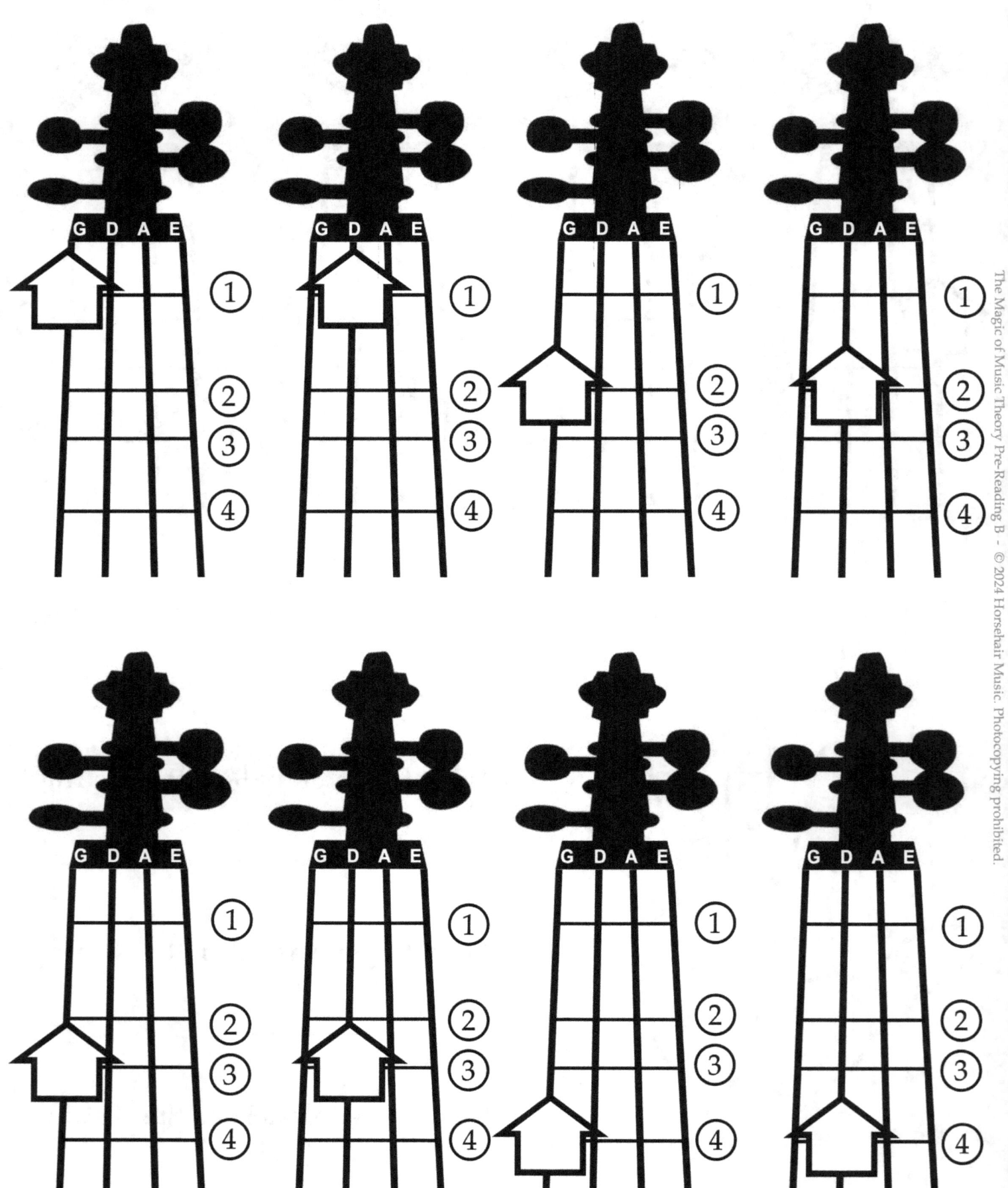

What do you hear? #4

Circle the letter of the string that you hear your teacher play.

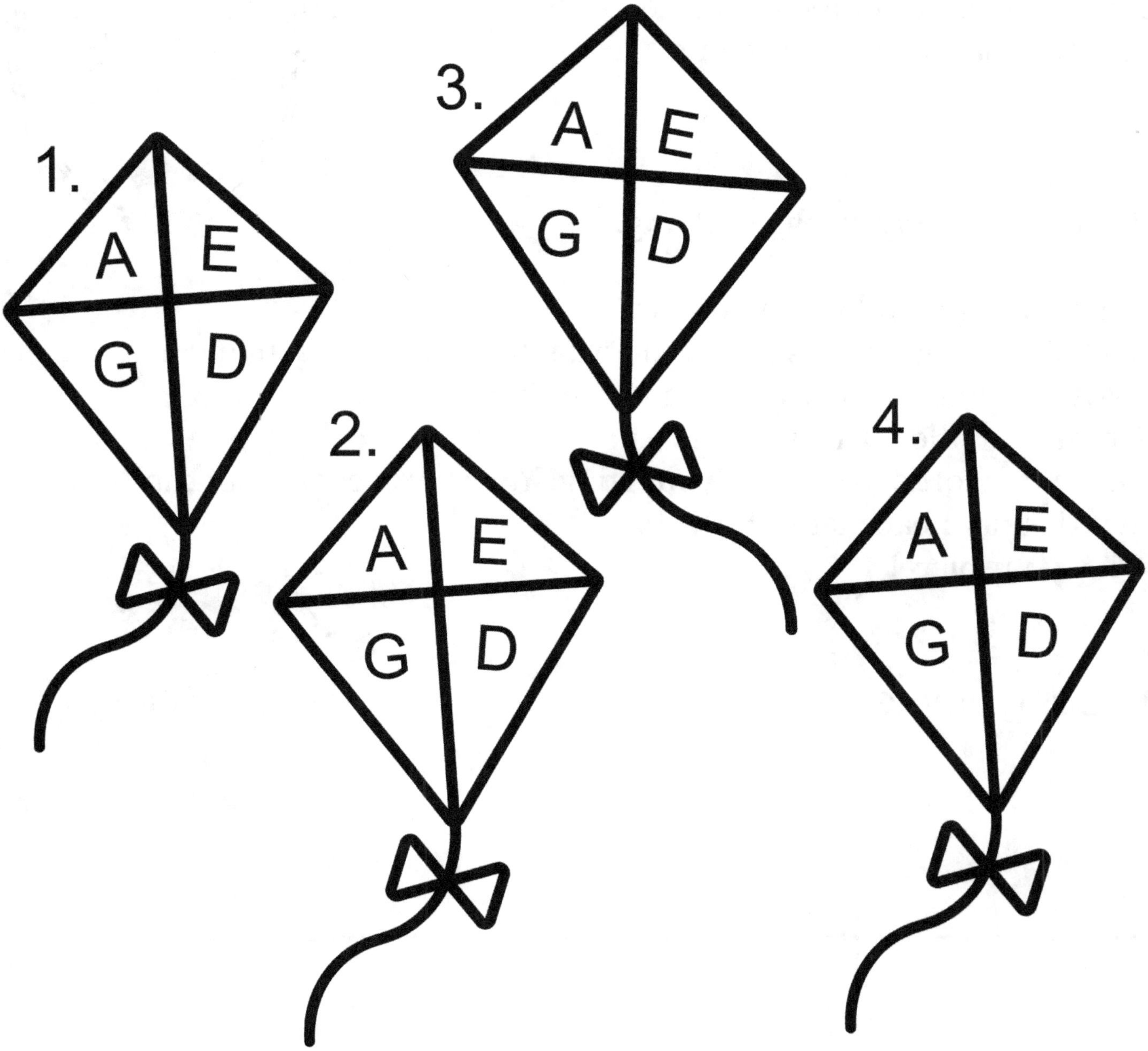

1.

2.

3.

4.

* For extra practice at identifying open strings, see page 80.

The teacher may choose from these examples:

Lesson 11

Johann Sebastian Bach [Bah-kuh} was a composer from Germany. He wrote a piece called *Air* that is over 5 minutes long! The entire piece is played only the G string! You get to compose a piece for the G string but it only has to be 9 notes long.

1. Compose a song on the G string.

1. We will begin and end on open G.
2. Pick 7 notes on the G string and write the letters on each line.
3. Write a dynamic for your song in the circle.
4. Think of a title for your song.
5. Make up words to go with your song. Your practice partner can write words under each letter for you.
6. Play your piece!

My Song Name:

_____

G   _____   _____   _____

Dynamic: ◯

_____   _____   _____   _____   G

2. Color the picture using the color guide in the square below.

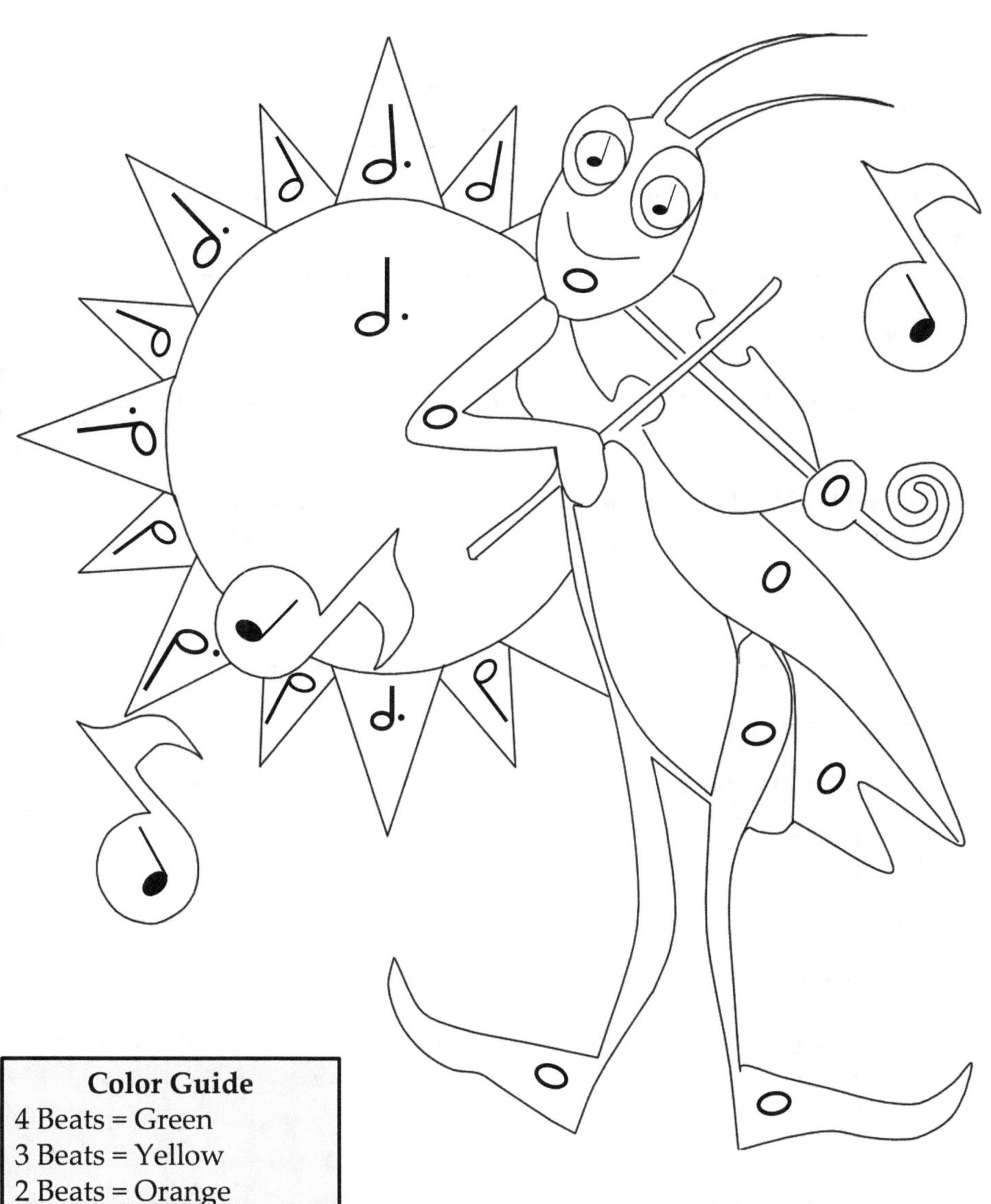

Color Guide
4 Beats = Green
3 Beats = Yellow
2 Beats = Orange
1 Beat = Black
Color the violin brown

Lesson 12

When a note is between 2 lines, we call it a space note. It touches the top and the bottom line but does not cross over either line.

Space Note

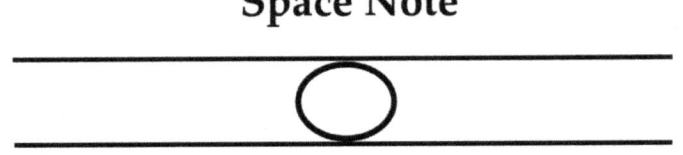

1. Trace 3 whole notes in the space. Then draw 1 more whole note space note.

To draw a note with a stem, draw the note head between the two lines, then draw a stem going up on the right.

2. Trace 3 dotted half note space notes. Then draw 1 more dotted half note space note. The dot always is on the right of the note head.

3. Trace 3 half note space notes. Then draw 1 more half note space note.

4. Trace 3 quarter notes. (Color them in!) Then draw 1 more quarter note space note.

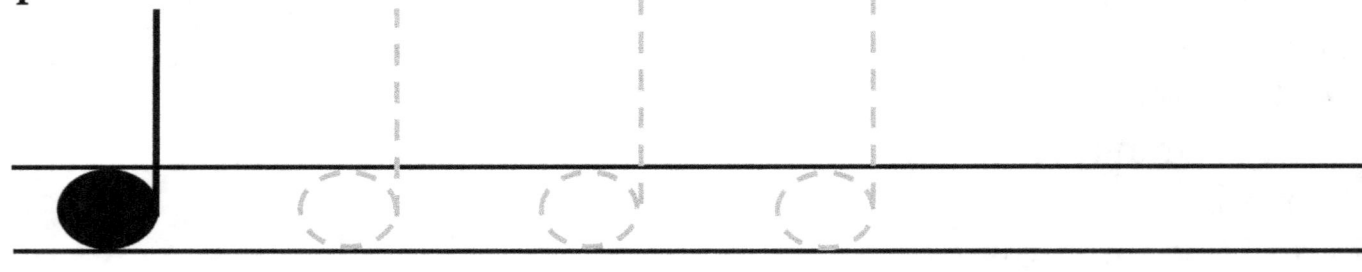

The Magic of Music Theory Pre-Reading B - © 2024 Horsehair Music. Photocopying prohibited.

When a line goes through the middle of a note, we call it a **line note**.

Line Note

5. Trace 3 whole note line notes. Then draw 1 more whole note line note.

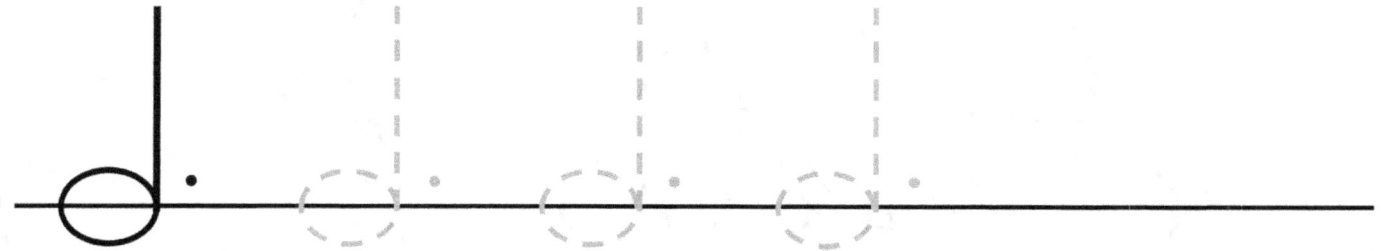

If the note has a stem, draw the note head with the line going through the middle. Then draw a stem going up on the right side. Place the dot on the right side of the note above the line.

6. Trace 3 dotted half notes. Then draw 1 more dotted half note line note.

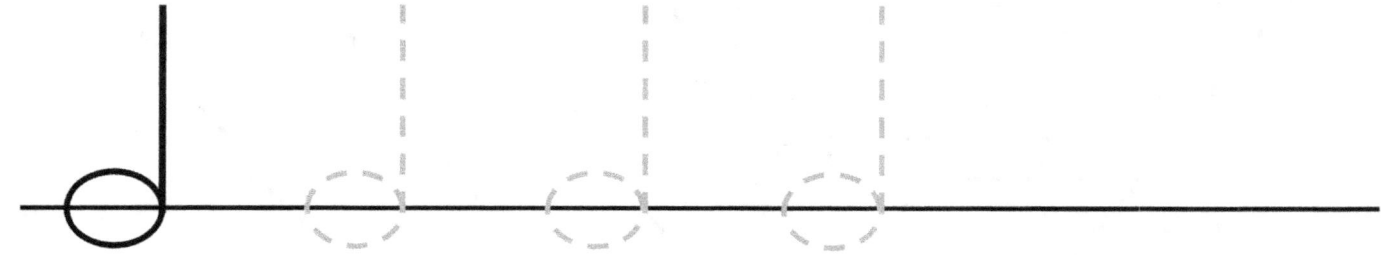

7. Trace 3 half notes. Then draw 1 more half note line note.

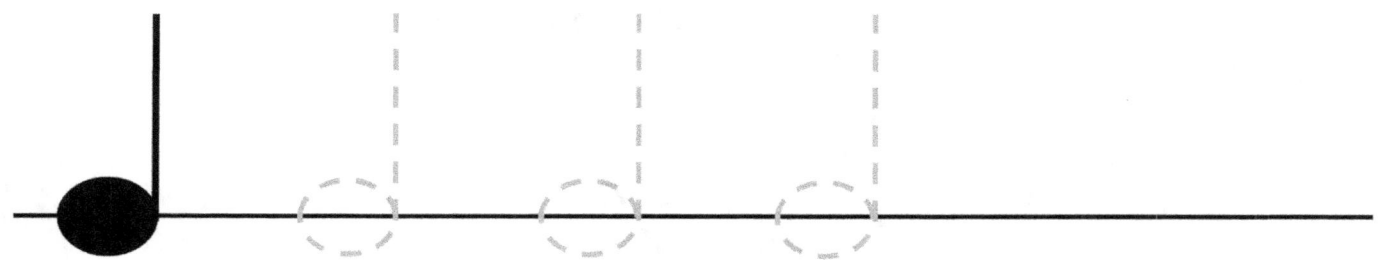

8. Trace 3 quarter notes and color them in. Then draw 1 more quarter note line note.

Line Note Maze

Help gemologist Gemma find the path to her next gem by following the line notes. Do not cross any space notes!

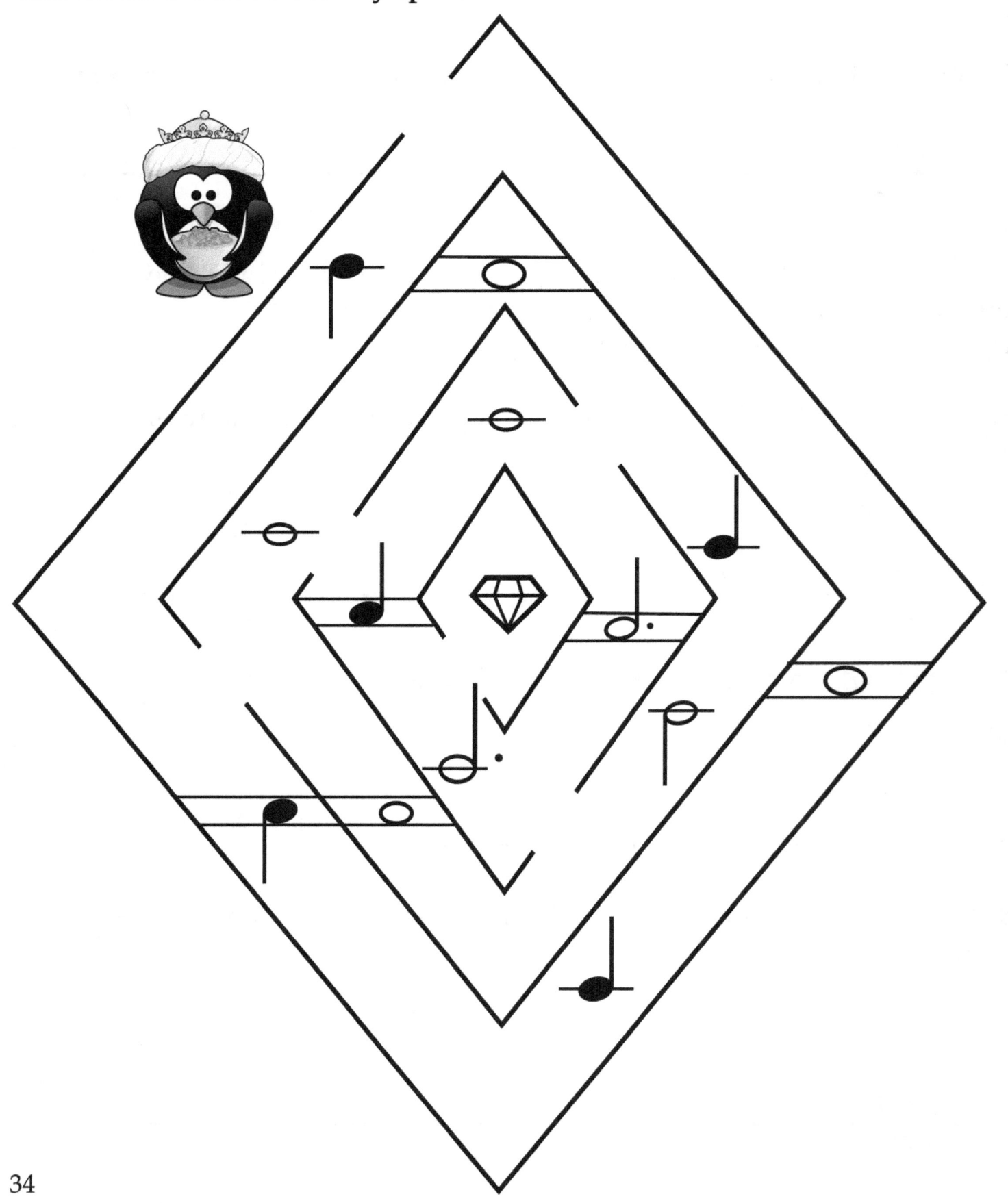

Lesson 13

When a quarter note doesn't make a sound, we say that it is resting. A **quarter rest** looks like a stretchy "z" with a "c" for a tail!

When you see a quarter rest, don't clap. Hold your hands open and quietly say "rest."

1. Clap these patterns and say their names.

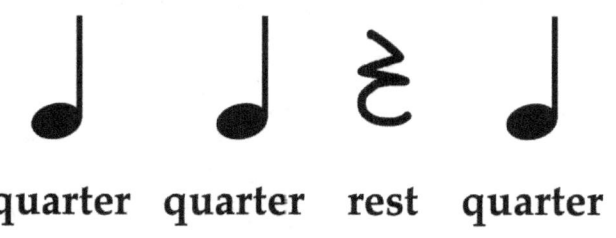

quarter   quarter   rest   quarter

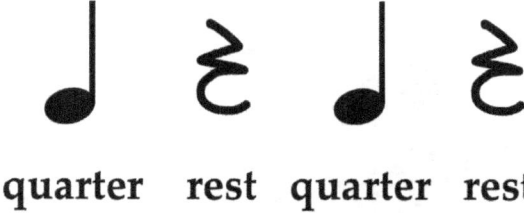

quarter   rest   quarter   rest

How to Draw a Quarter Rest

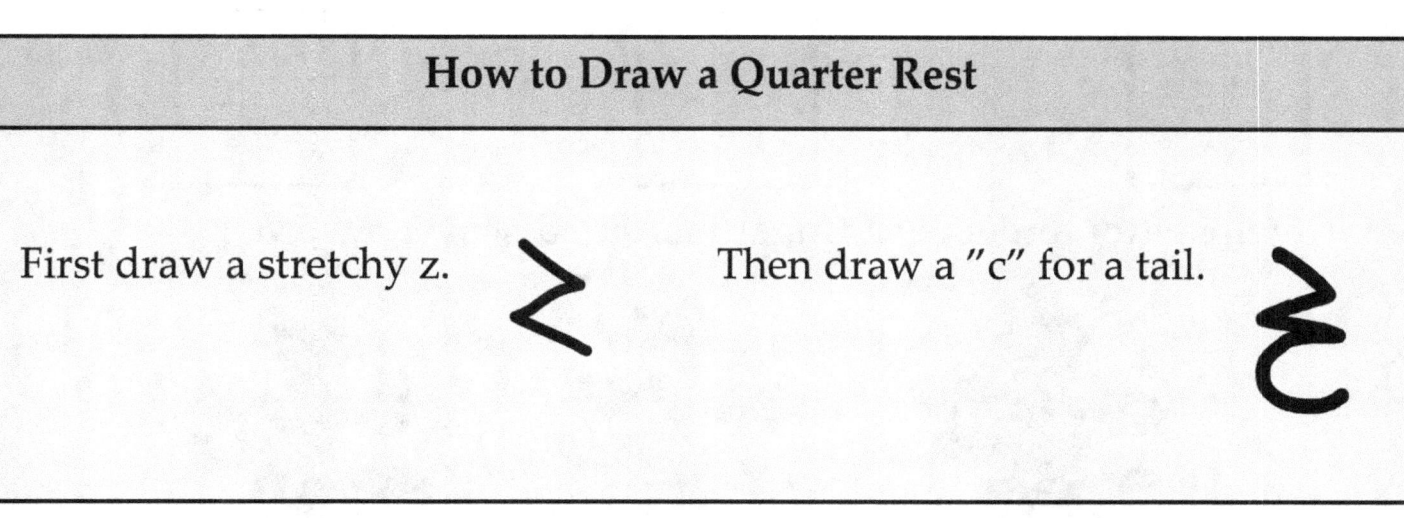

First draw a stretchy z.

Then draw a "c" for a tail.

2. Trace the 3 quarter rests.

3. Draw a quarter rest in the box.

4. Circle whether each note is a line note or a space note.

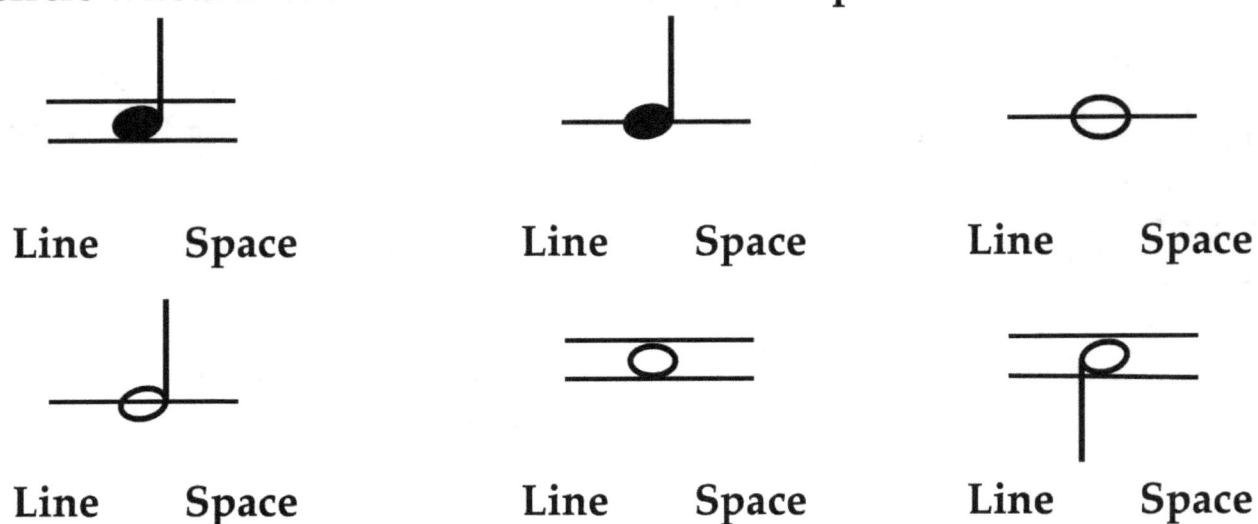

Line Space	Line Space	Line Space

Line Space	Line Space	Line Space

5. Write the dynamic letter for each picture in the box: *f*, *mf*, or *p*.

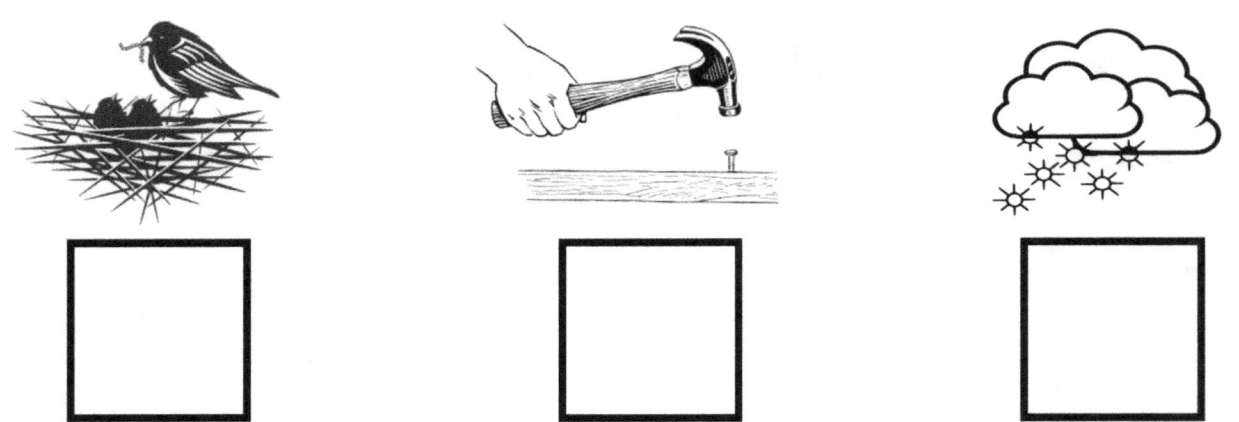

6. Write the letter under each fingerboard to discover a word.

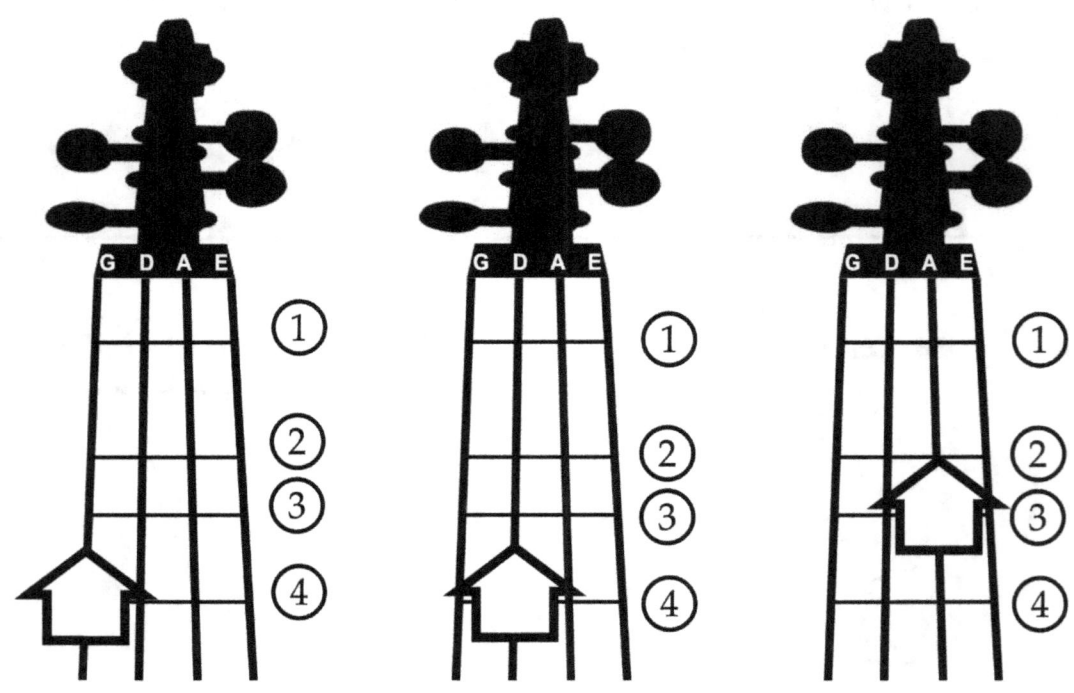

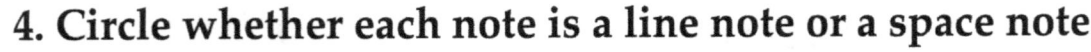

Pick A Daisy

Pick A Daisy

G String Game

2 Players

What you need:
   2 cups (optional)
   5 pennies
   5 dimes
   1 die

How to play:

1. Each player chooses the type of coin he wants to use, pennies or dimes.
2. Place your coins in a pile or a cup near the game board.
3. Take turns rolling the die. The number on the die is a finger number. Place a coin on the flower that matches the G string letter for the finger number rolled.
4. The first player to place all his coins on the game board wins.
5. If you roll and there is no letter that matches that finger, the next player takes a turn.

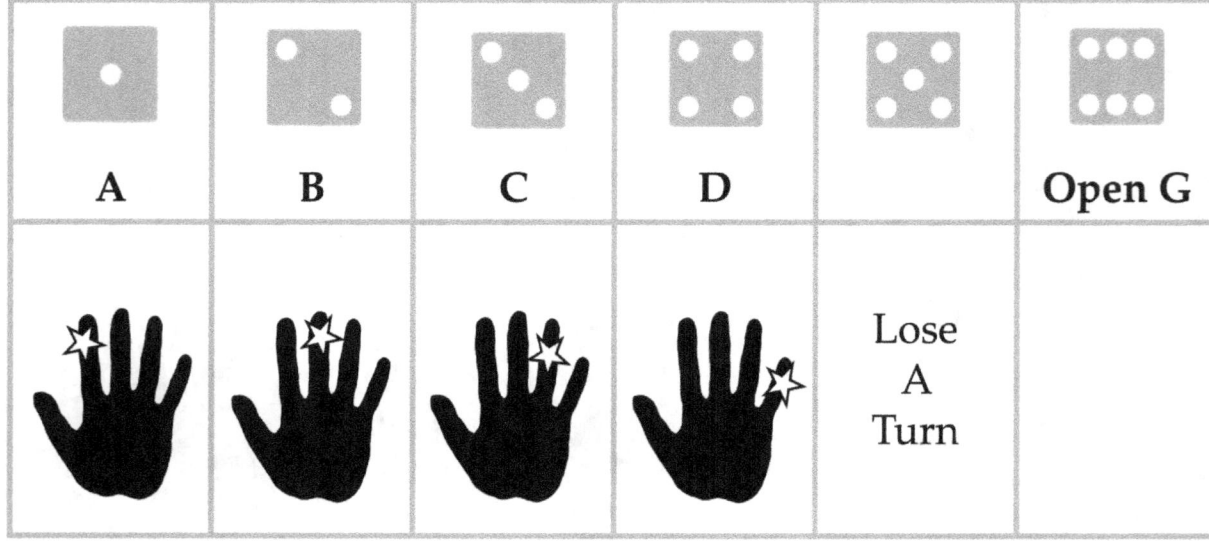

A	B	C	D		Open G
				Lose A Turn	

Lesson 14

 The **whole rest** and the **half rest** use the same shape!

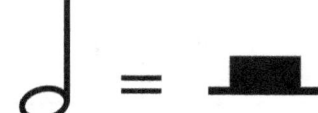

The **half rest** is a like a hat.   The **whole rest** is like a hole to plant a tree.

half-rest

1-2

whole-rest-4-beats

1-2-3-4

Because rests are silent, don't clap for rests! Hold your hands  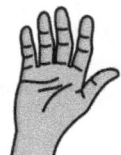 open facing up and whisper the counts for each rest.

1. Clap each line and say the beats.

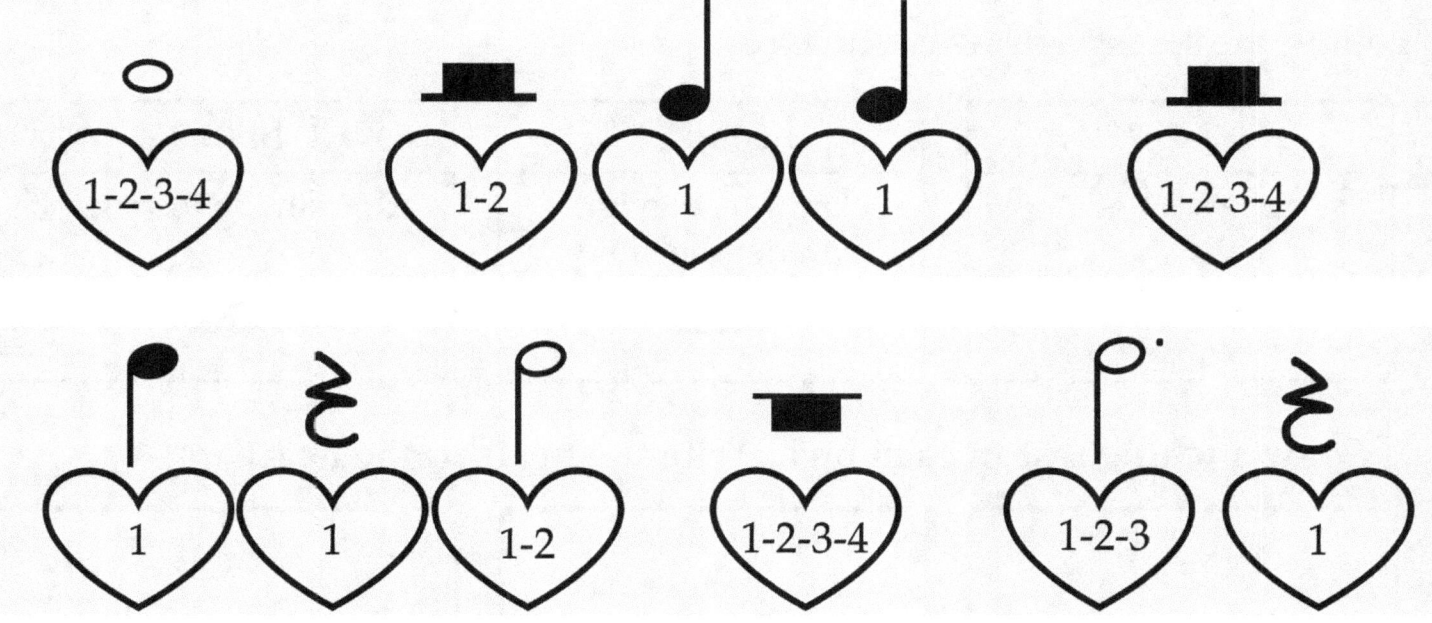

1-2-3-4   1-2   1   1   1-2-3-4

1   1   1-2   1-2-3-4   1-2-3   1

2. Draw a line from the note to the matching rest.

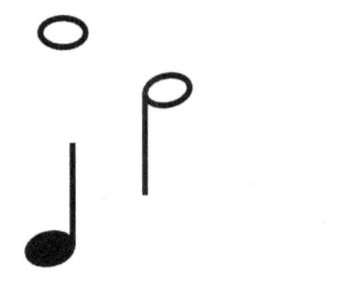      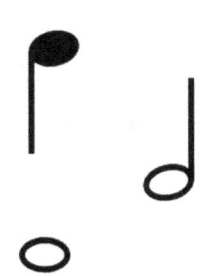

Lesson 15

Follow the steps to draw a half rest.

Step 1	Step 2	Step 3
Draw a line.	Draw a rectangle under the line.	Color in the rectangle.
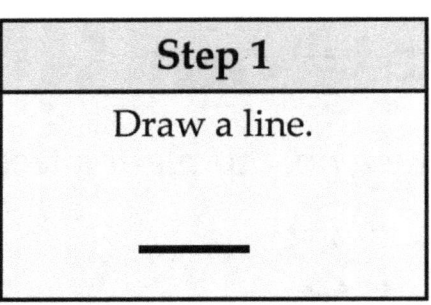		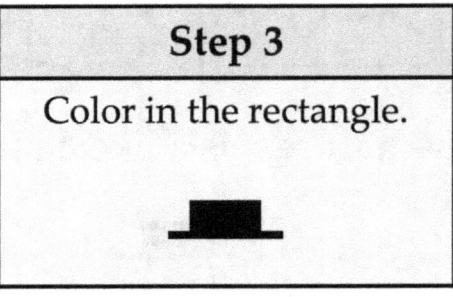

1. Draw a half rest in each box. Write the half rest beats in each heart.

Follow the steps to draw a whole rest.

Step 1	Step 2	Step 3
Draw a line.	Draw a rectangle under the line.	Color in the rectangle.
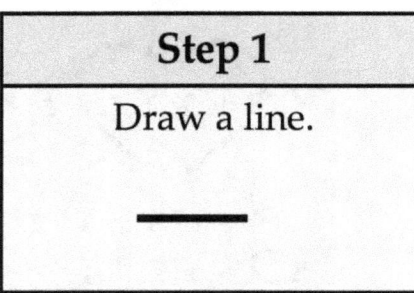		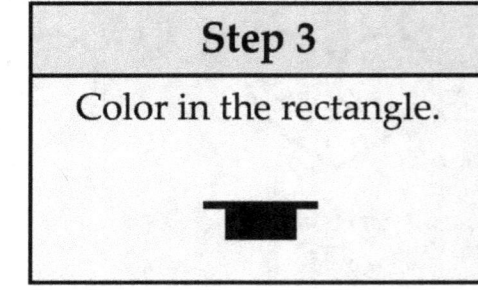

2. Draw a whole rest in each box. Write the beats in the heart.

3. The dentist is checking to see how many teeth these kids have lost. lost. In the tooth draw *the note* that matches the number of teeth each kid has lost.

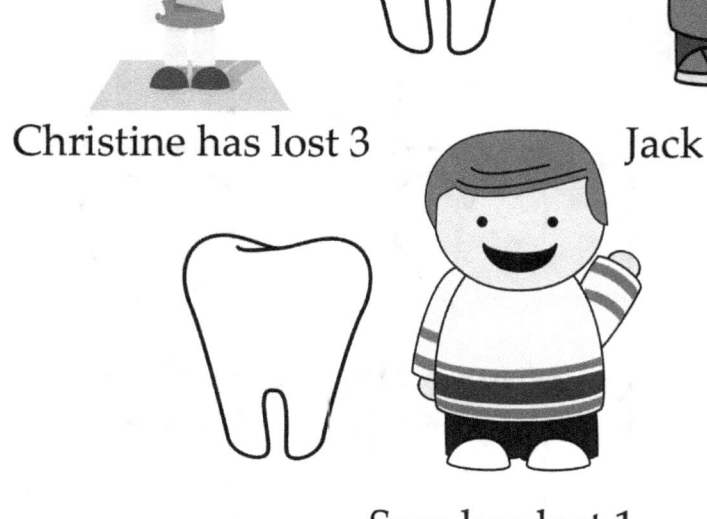

Christine has lost 3

Jack has lost 2

Sam has lost 1

Mallory has lost 4

2. These kids are still waiting to lose a tooth. In each tooth draw a *rest* for the number of wiggly teeth they have!

Lucy has 1 wiggly tooth

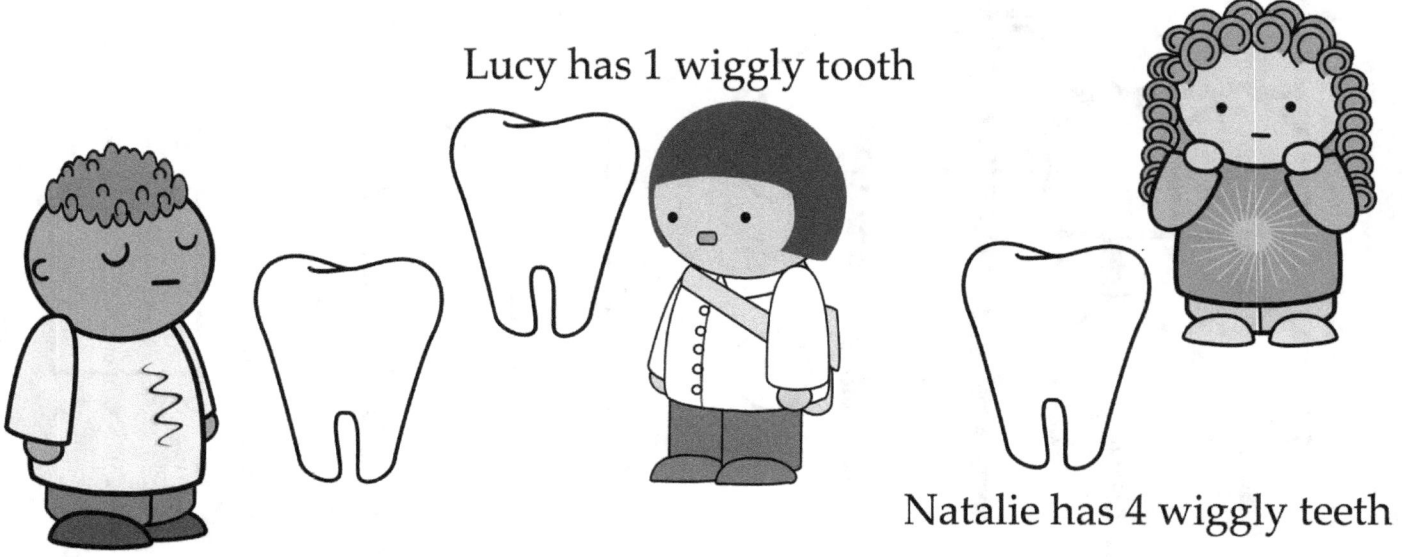

Jamal has 2 wiggly teeth

Natalie has 4 wiggly teeth

3. In the tooth, use a note(s) to draw the number of teeth that you have lost!

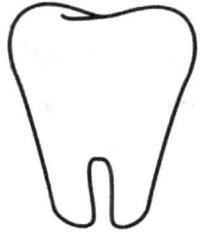

Lesson 16

1. Write the letter name in the houses and the finger number in the circles.

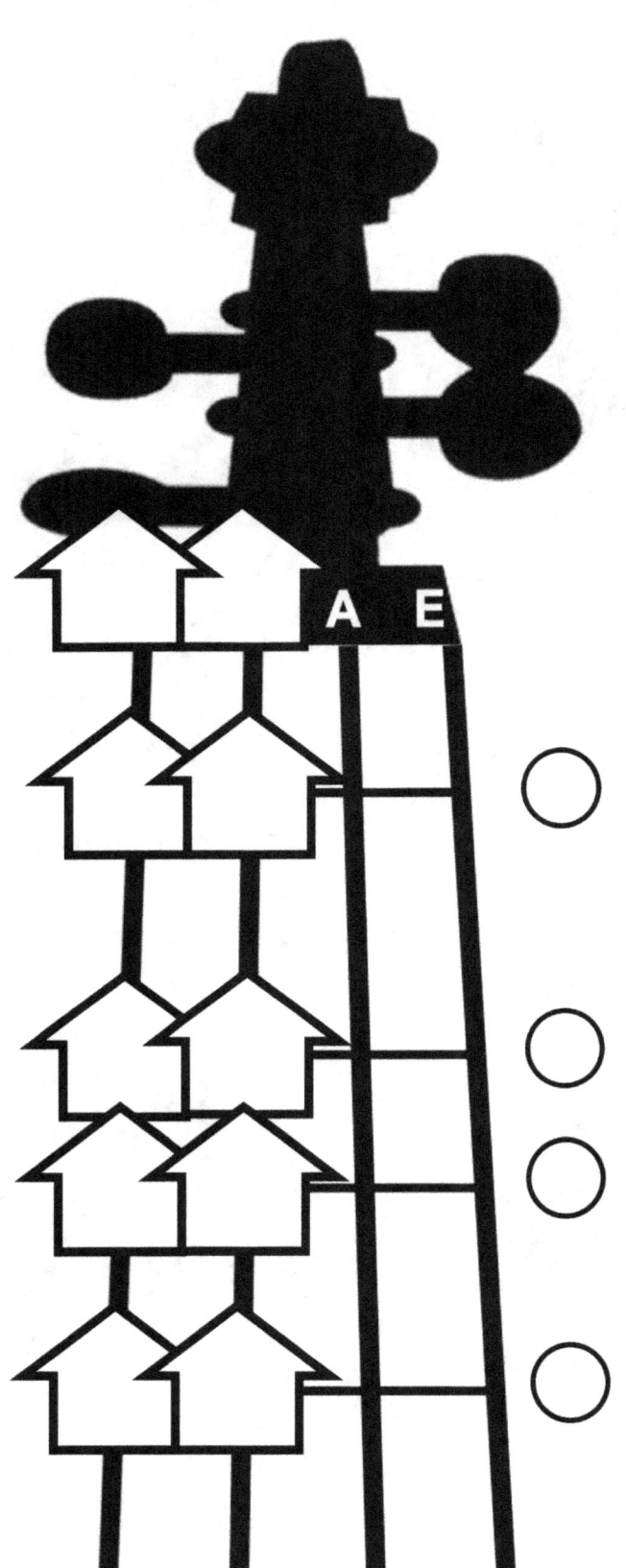

3. Your practice partner will place a coin on a house. Using your violin, play Mississippi Stop Stop on the covered note.

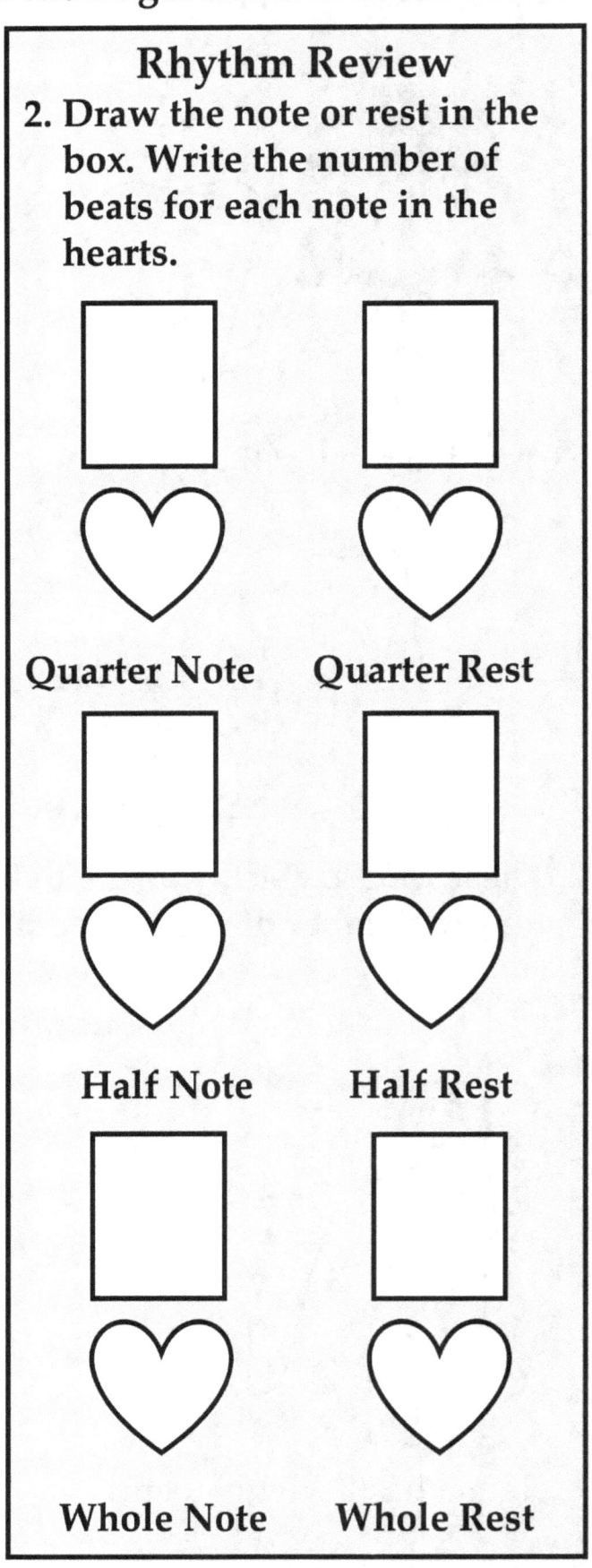

Rhythm Review

2. Draw the note or rest in the box. Write the number of beats for each note in the hearts.

Quarter Note	**Quarter Rest**
Half Note	**Half Rest**
Whole Note	**Whole Rest**

4. Fill in the D string letters stepping up and stepping down.

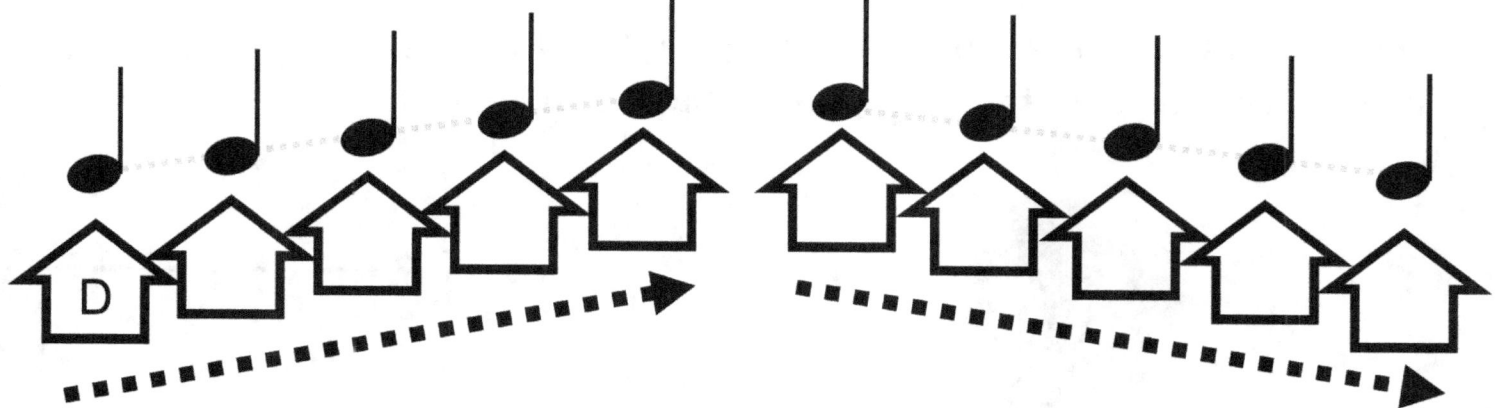

5. Fill in the G string letters stepping up and stepping down.

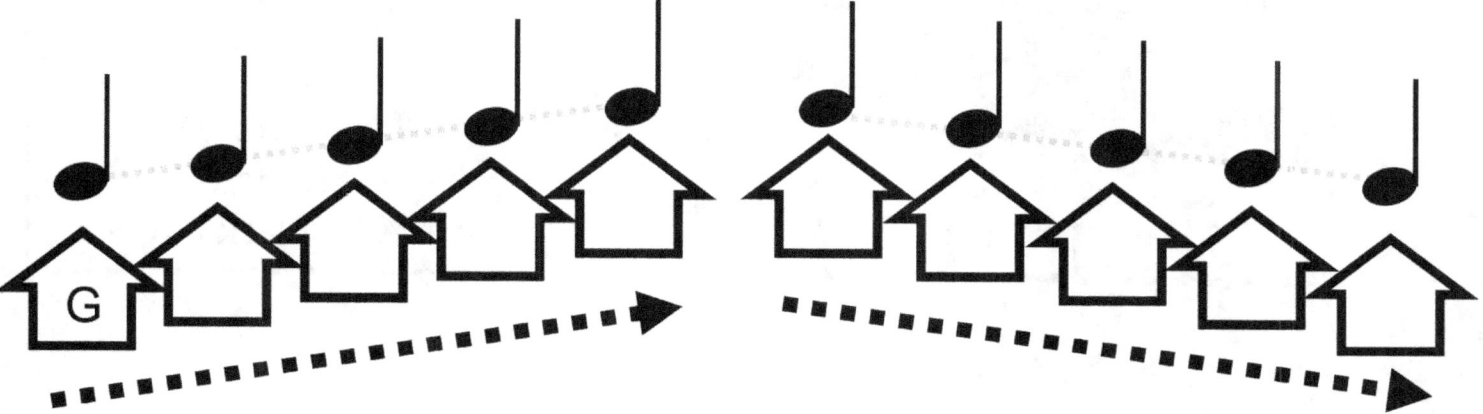

6. Look at each box and draw an X through the thing that does not belong in that box.

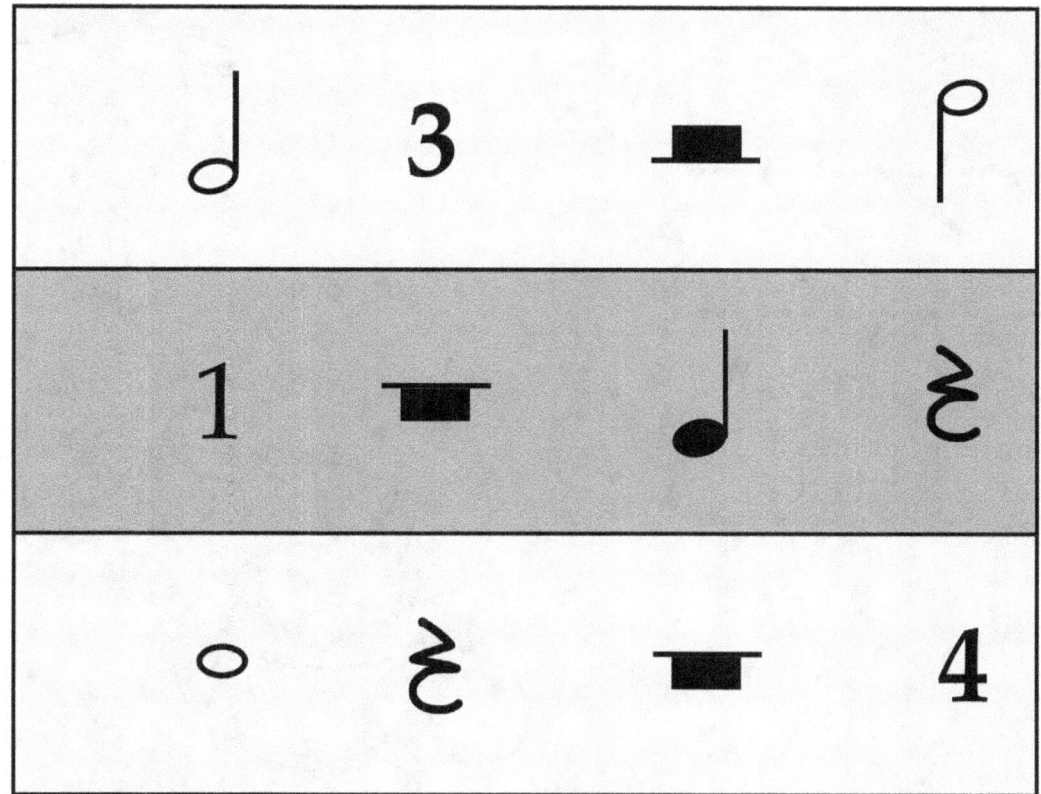

Lesson 17

1. It's a neighborhood house painting party! Follow the color guide and color each house on the fingerboard the correct color!

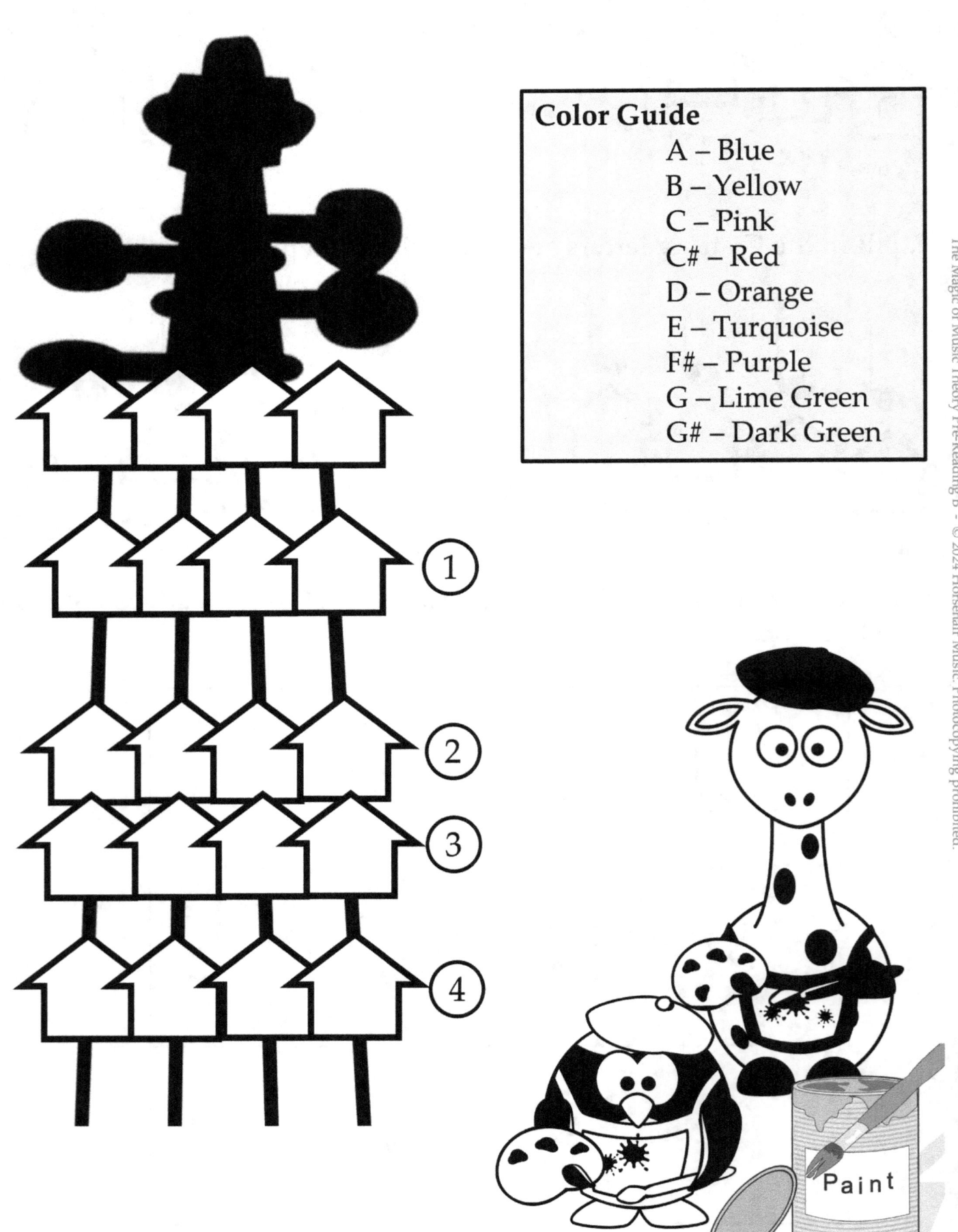

Color Guide
- A – Blue
- B – Yellow
- C – Pink
- C# – Red
- D – Orange
- E – Turquoise
- F# – Purple
- G – Lime Green
- G# – Dark Green

What do you hear? #5

Color the egg of the open string that you hear.

1.

G D A E

2.

G D A E

3.

G D A E

4.

G D A E

* For extra practice at identifying open strings, see page 80.

The teacher may choose from these examples:

Lesson 18

Rhythm is when we organize notes into groups. Each group must have the same number of beats. We draw a line between each group called a **bar line**. The space in between the bar lines is called a **measure**. A **double bar line** is a thin line next to a thick line. The thin line always comes first, before the thick line. A double bar line shows the end of a piece.

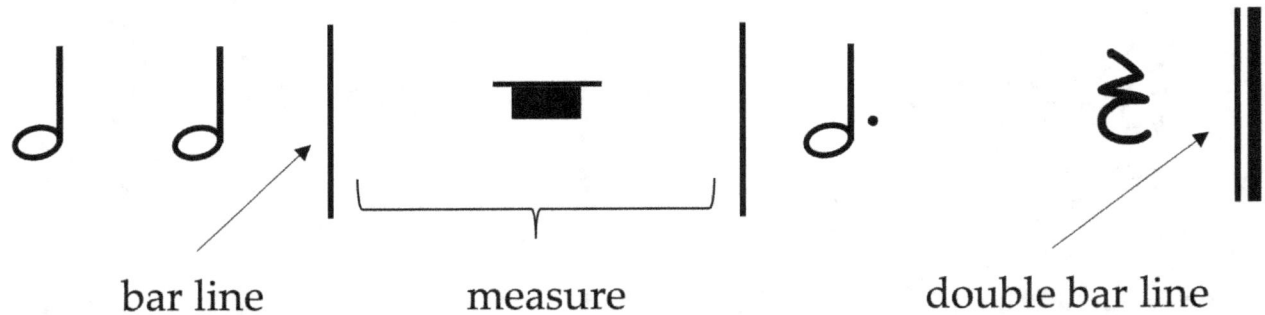

bar line   measure   double bar line

1. **Circle the bar lines.**
2. **Draw a box around the measures**
3. **Draw a triangle around the double bar lines.**

The Magic of Music Theory Pre-Reading B - © 2024 Horsehair Music. Photocopying prohibited.

4. Circle the notes and rests you find hidden in the picture.

African Adventure

Lesson 19

1. Write the number beats for each note or rest.

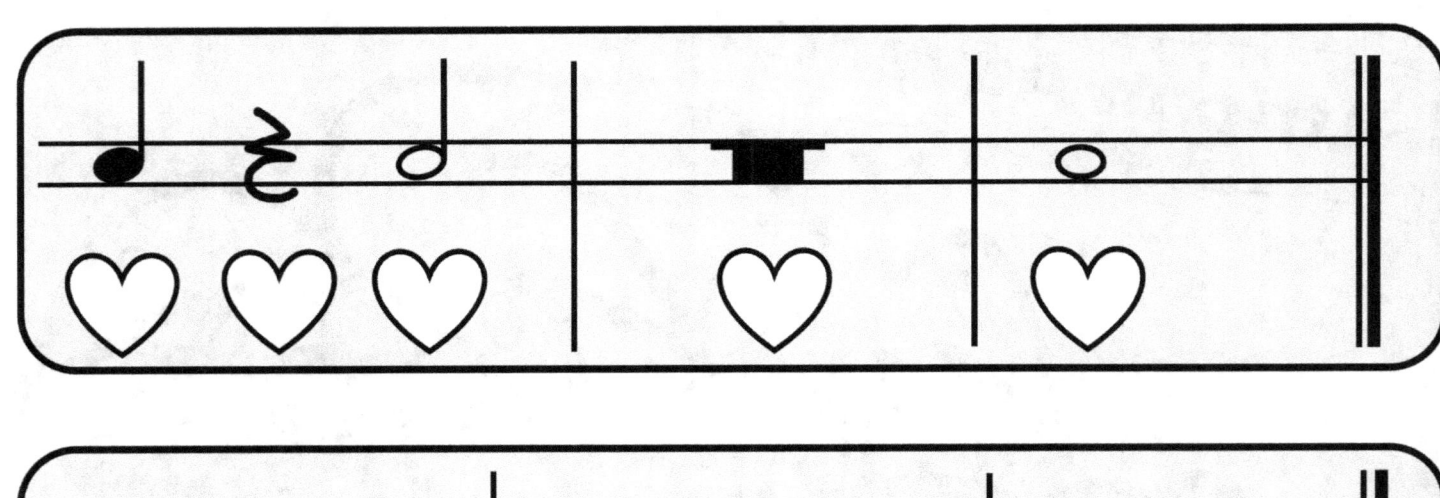

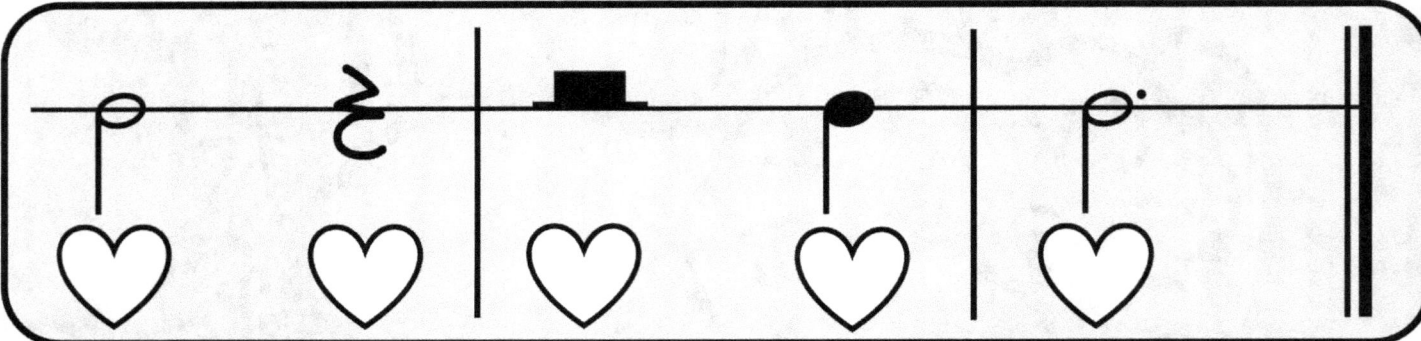

2. Draw line notes above each heart that match the number of beats.

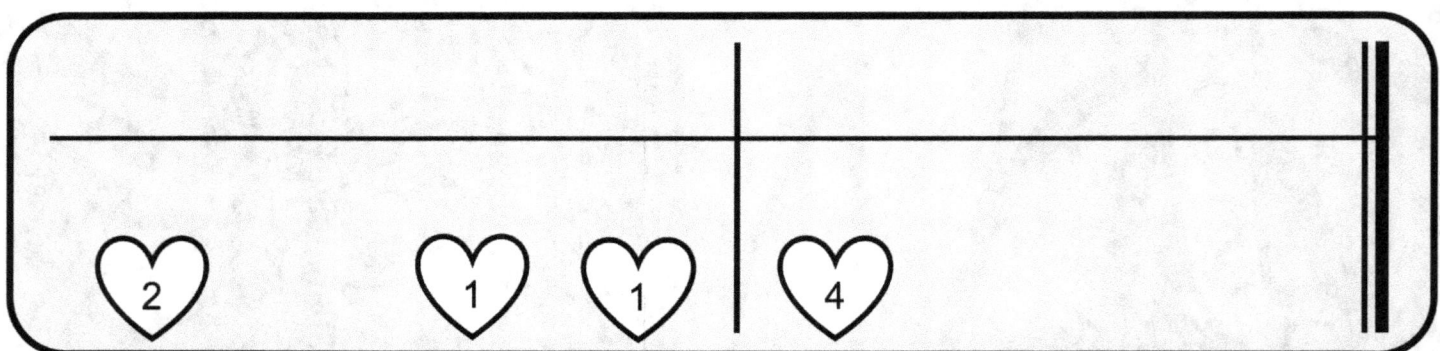

3. Draw space notes above each heart that match the number of beats.

Lesson 20

A **time signature** is two numbers stacked on top of each other at the beginning of a piece. The most **common time signature** used in music is four, four. The top number of the time signature tells how many beats are in each measure. To read a time signature, we say the top number first, then the bottom number. We say the time signature below "four, four."

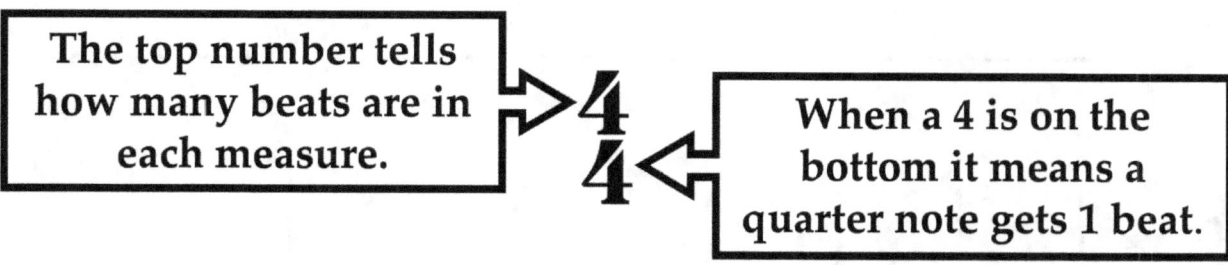

The top number tells how many beats are in each measure. ⟹ 4/4 ⟸ **When a 4 is on the bottom it means a quarter note gets 1 beat.**

To count the beats in each measure, give one number to every beat.

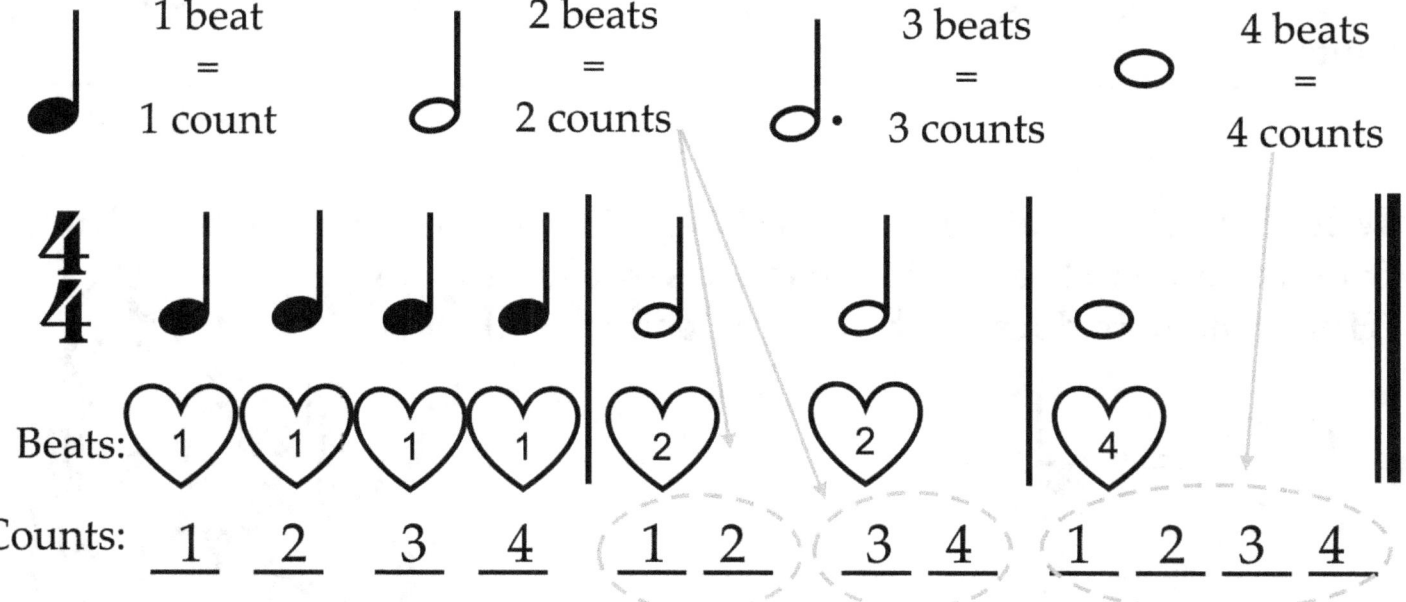

1 beat = 1 count   2 beats = 2 counts   3 beats = 3 counts   4 beats = 4 counts

Beats: 1 1 1 1 | 2 | 2 | 4

Counts: 1 2 3 4 (1 2) (3 4) (1 2 3 4)

1. Count the beats in each measure.

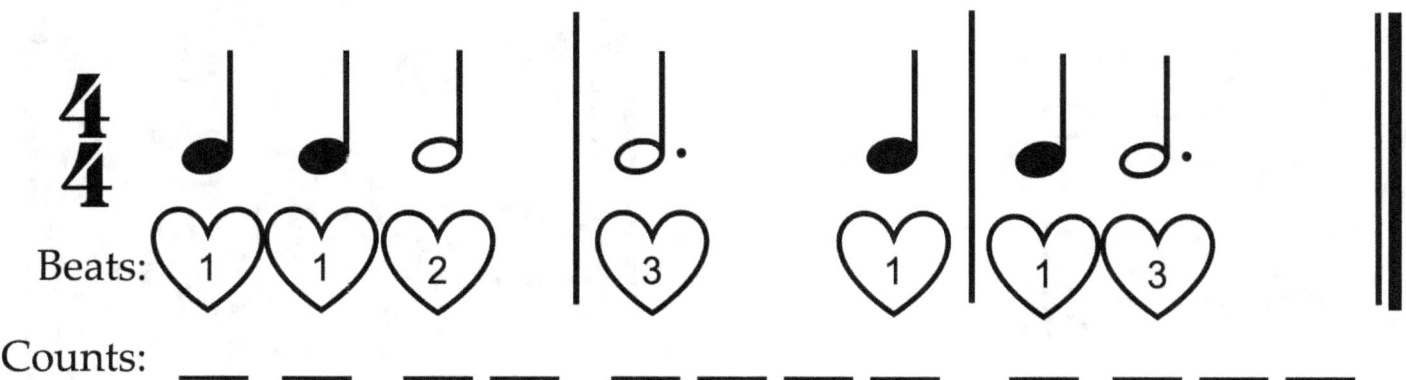

Beats: 1 1 2 | 3 | 1 | 1 3

Counts: __ __ __ __ __ __ __ __ __

2. Write the beats for each note in the heart. Then count the beats.

Beats:

Counts: __ __ __ __   __ __ __   __ __ __ __   __ __ __ __

Beats:

Counts: __ __ __ __   __ __ __ __   __ __ __ __

3. Write the number of beats for each note in the heart. Then draw a line from the note to the rest that has the same number of beats. (Hint: One note does not have a matching rest.)

♡ = ♩

♡ = 𝅗𝅥

♡ = 𝅝

♡ = 𝅗𝅥.

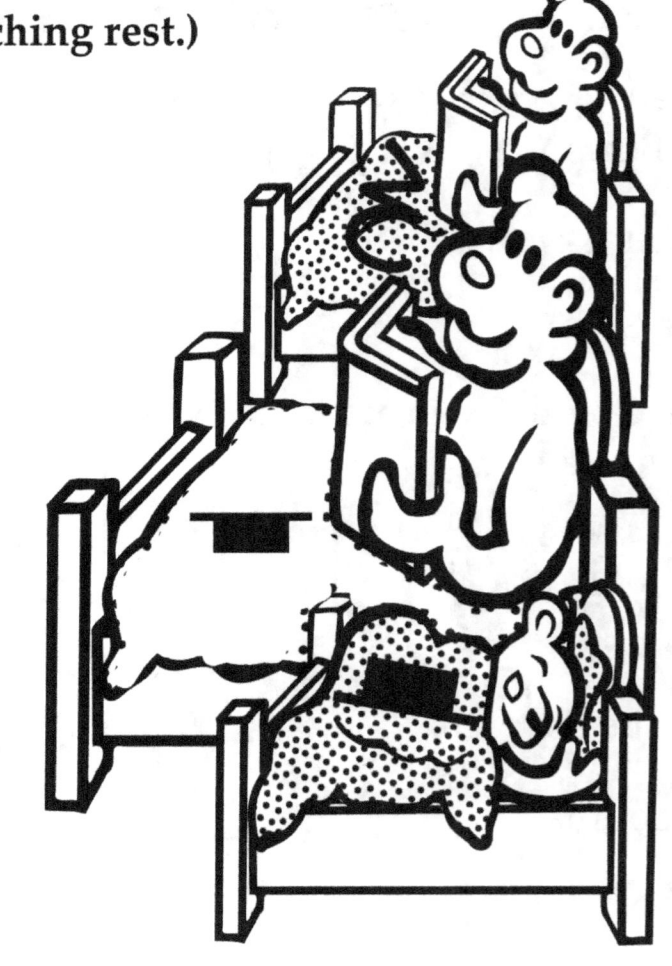

Lesson 21

We count rests the same way we count notes. A quarter rest says to rest for 1 beat. So, it will get 1 count. A half rest says to rest for 2 beats. It will get 2 counts. A whole rest says to rest for 4 beats. It will get 4 counts.

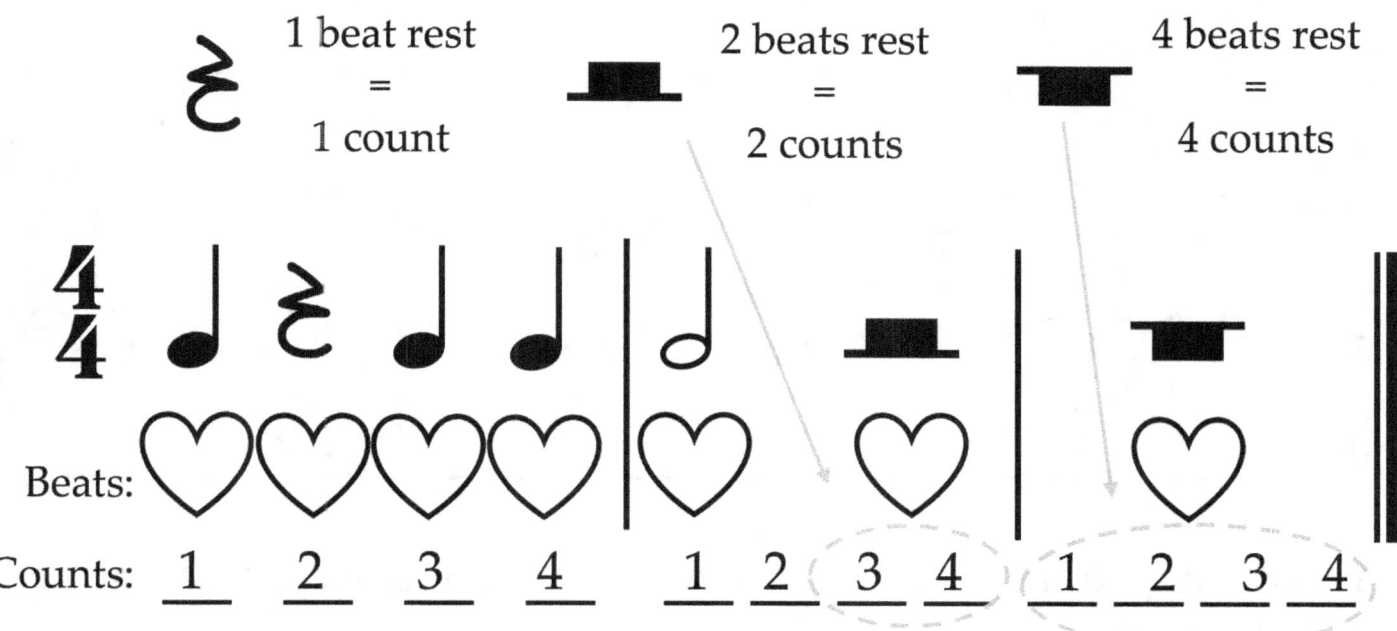

1. Write the beats in the heart for each note or rest. Then write the counts for each measure on the lines.

2. Write the beats for each note in the heart. Then count the beats.

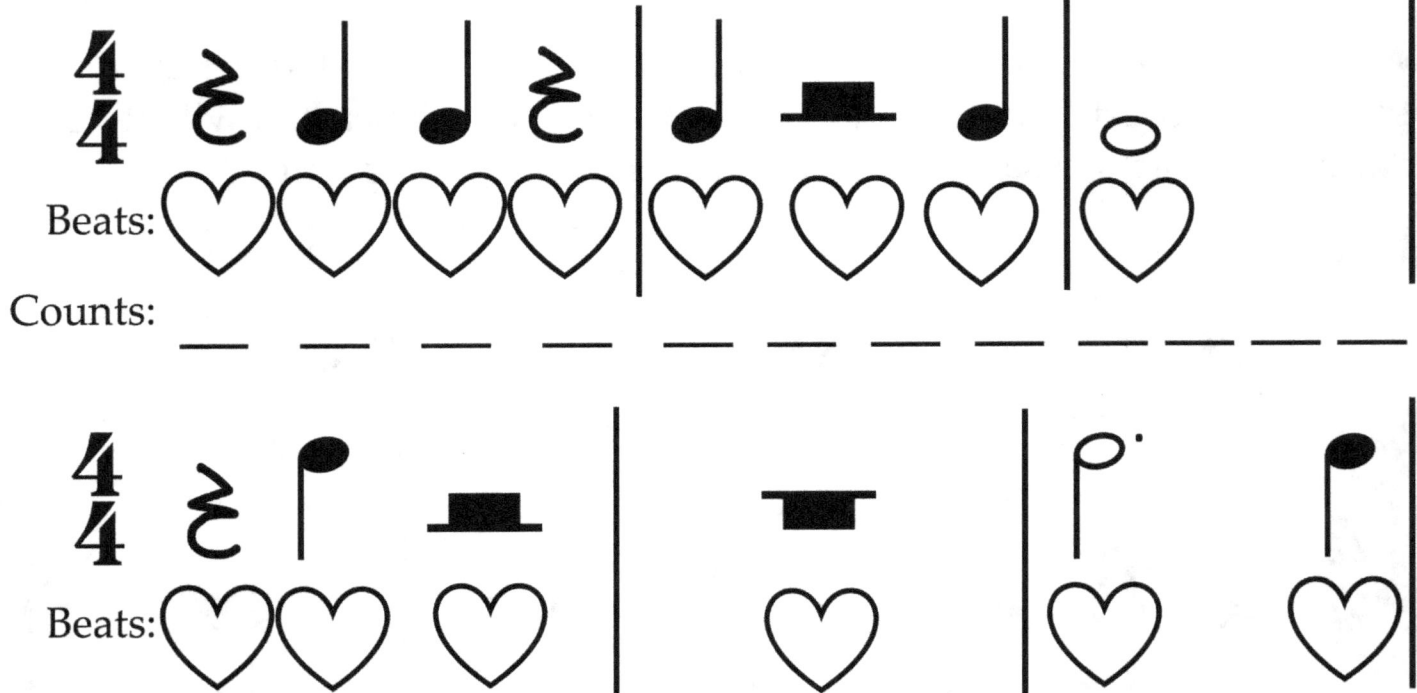

Beats:

Counts: __ __ __ __ __ __ __ __ __

Beats:

Counts: __ __ __ __ __ __ __ __ __

3. Fingerboard words: Color in the house on the fingerboard that matches the letter at the end of each string.

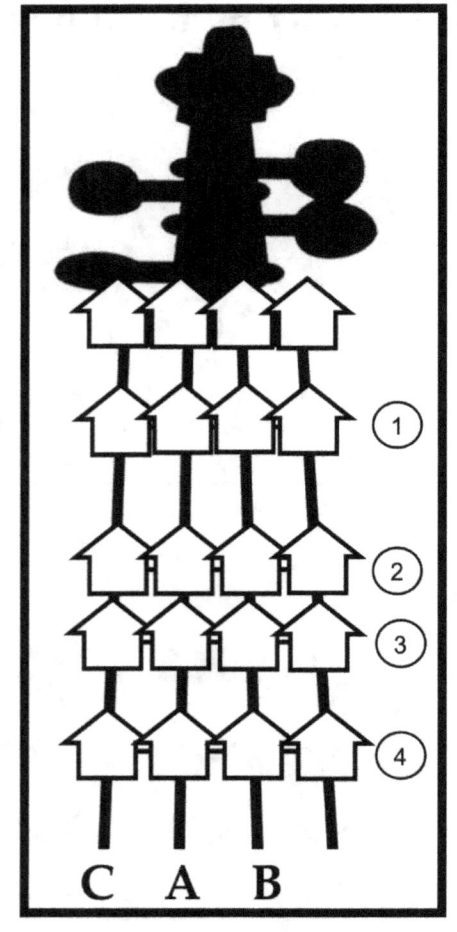

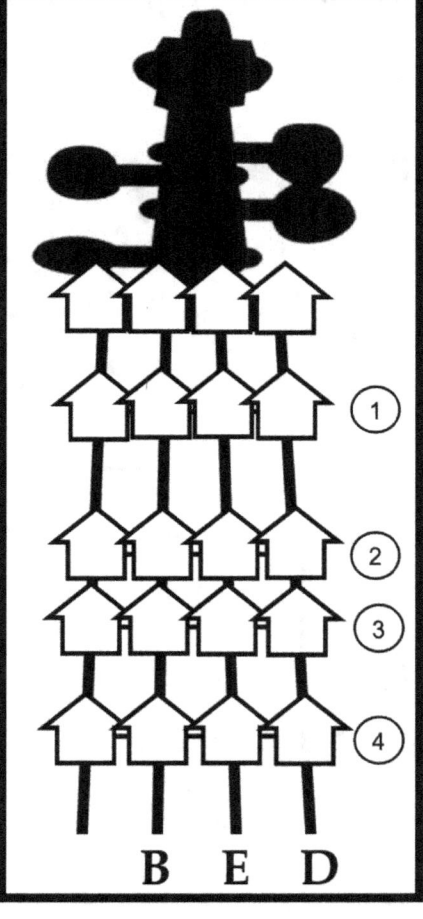

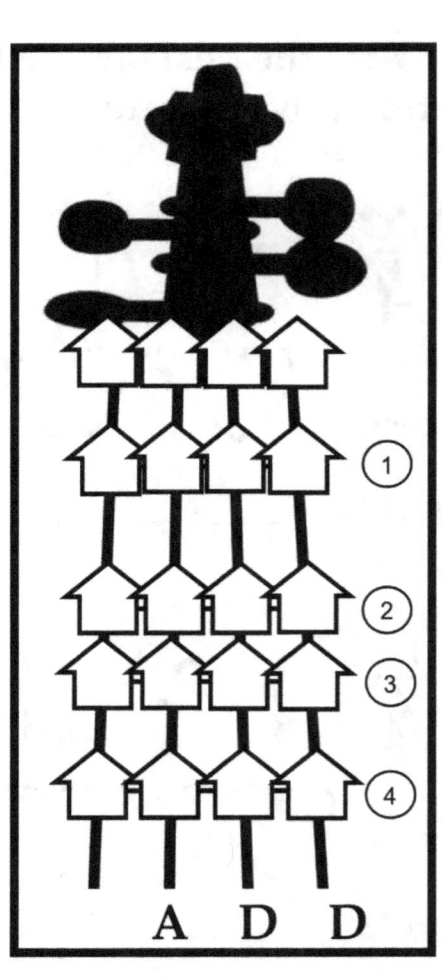

C A B

B E D

A D D

The Magic of Music Theory Pre-Reading B - © 2024 Horsehair Music. Photocopying prohibited.

Lesson 22

The top number of the time signature tells how many beats are in each measure. Any number can be the top number of a time signature. Remember a *4 on the bottom means a quarter note gets 1 beat.*

1. Circle the top numbers of each time signature.

$$\frac{4}{4} \qquad \frac{2}{4} \qquad \frac{3}{4} \qquad \frac{5}{4} \qquad \frac{6}{4}$$

If 3 is the top number of the time signature, then each measure will have 3 beats. You will count to 3 in each measure.

2. Write the beats for each note in the heart and the counts on the lines.

Beats:

Counts: __ __ __ __ __ __ __ __ __ __ __ __

If 2 is the top number of the time signature, then each measure will have 2 beats. You will count to 2 in each measure.

3. Write the beats for each note in the heart and the counts on the lines.

Beats:

Counts: __ __ __ __ __ __

53

If 5 is the top number of the time signature, then each measure will have 5 beats. You will count to 5 in each measure.

3. Write the beats for each note in the heart and the counts on the lines.

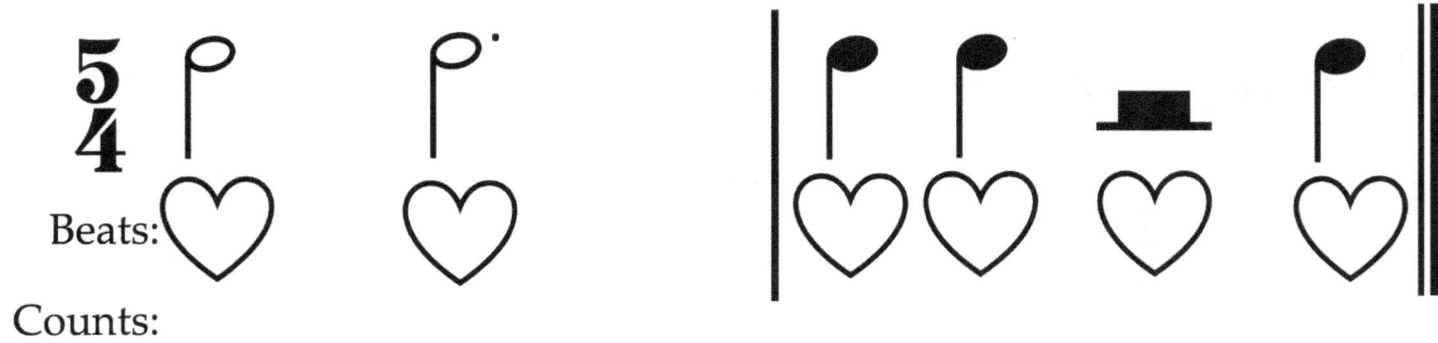

Beats:

Counts: ___ ___ ___ ___ ___ ___ ___ ___ ___ ___

4. Write the counts on the lines. Then draw bar lines.

Beats: 3 | 1 | 1 | 1 | 1 | 1 | 2 | 2

Counts: ___ ___ ___ ___ ___ ___ ___ ___ ___ ___ ___

5. Circle if the notes step up, step down, or stay the same.

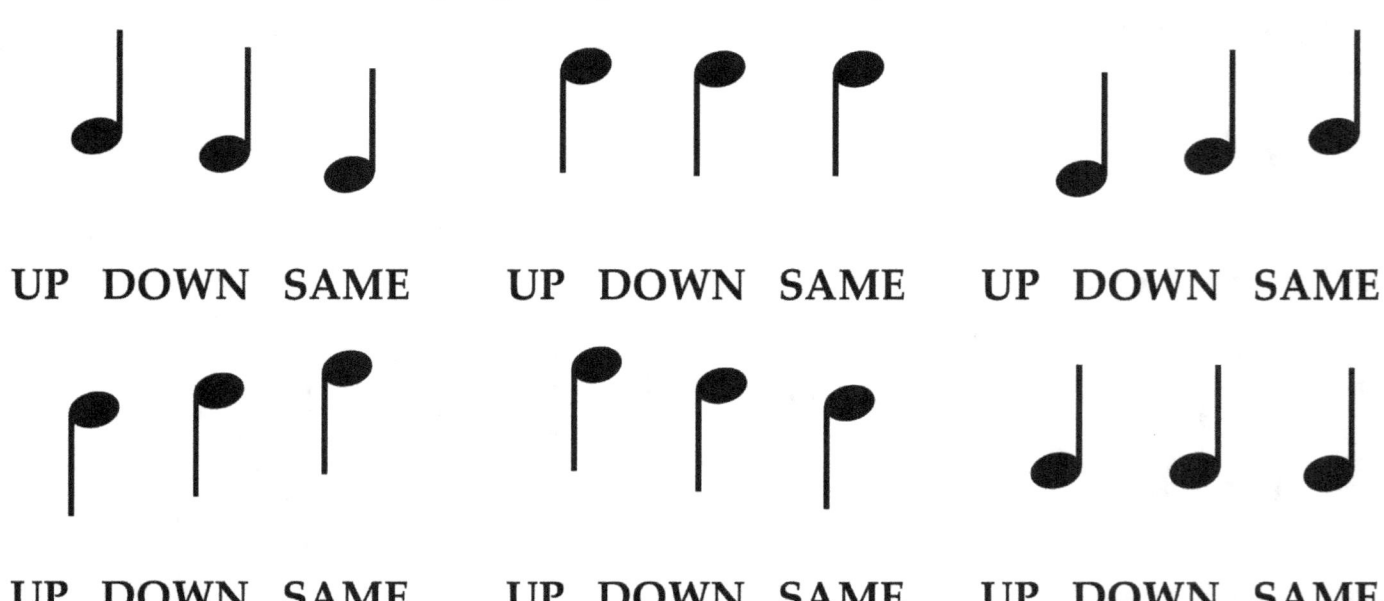

UP   DOWN   SAME   UP   DOWN   SAME   UP   DOWN   SAME

UP   DOWN   SAME   UP   DOWN   SAME   UP   DOWN   SAME

6. Each paint splat is a measure. Count the number of beats in each splat. Write the number for the time signature in the box.

55

WET PAINT!

2 Players

What you need:
  1 die
  2 cups
  5 pennies
  5 dimes

First have the student fill in the missing top number of the time signature. (Each paint blob is 1 measure.)

- Each player takes turns rolling the die.
- The player who rolled the die places a coin on the paint blob that has the same number of beats as what he/she rolled. It doesn't matter if the other player has a coin on that blob.
- If the player already has a coin on the blob, his/her turn is over.
- The first player to have a coin on all the blobs wins.

The Magic of Music Theory Pre-Reading B - © 2024 Horsehair Music. Photocopying prohibited.

Lesson 23

A whole rest means to rest for 4 beats, but it can also mean to rest for a whole measure!

1. Write the beats for each *rest* in the heart. Write the counts for each measure on the lines.

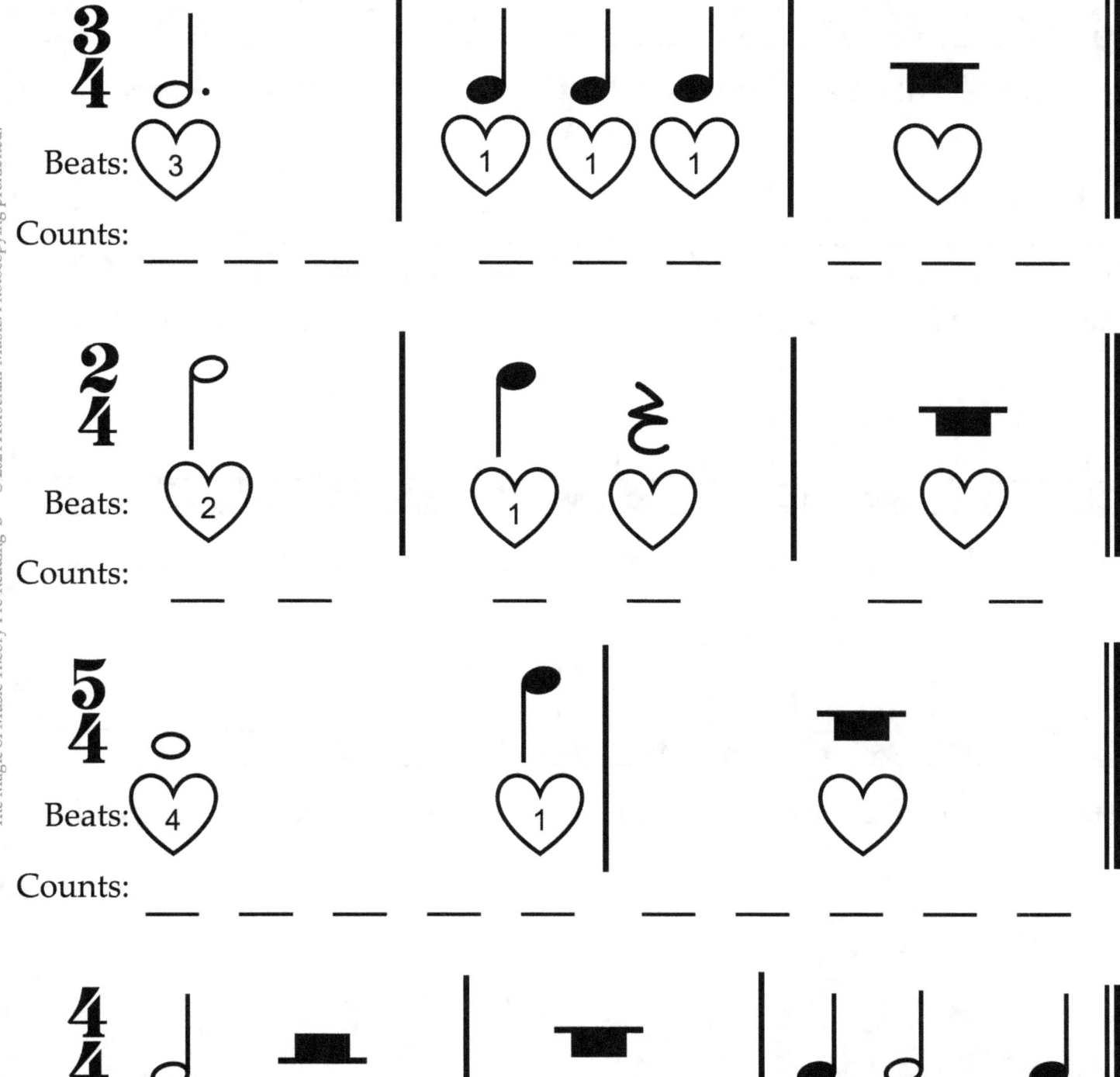

2. This song is missing bar lines. Look at the time signature. Then draw in the bar lines. Draw a double bar line at the end.

Six Little Ducks

Lesson 24

Music notes are written on a **staff.** The staff is made up of **5 lines** and **4 spaces**. Always start counting the lines on the bottom line and move up.

1. Write the line numbers in each star beginning from the bottom line.

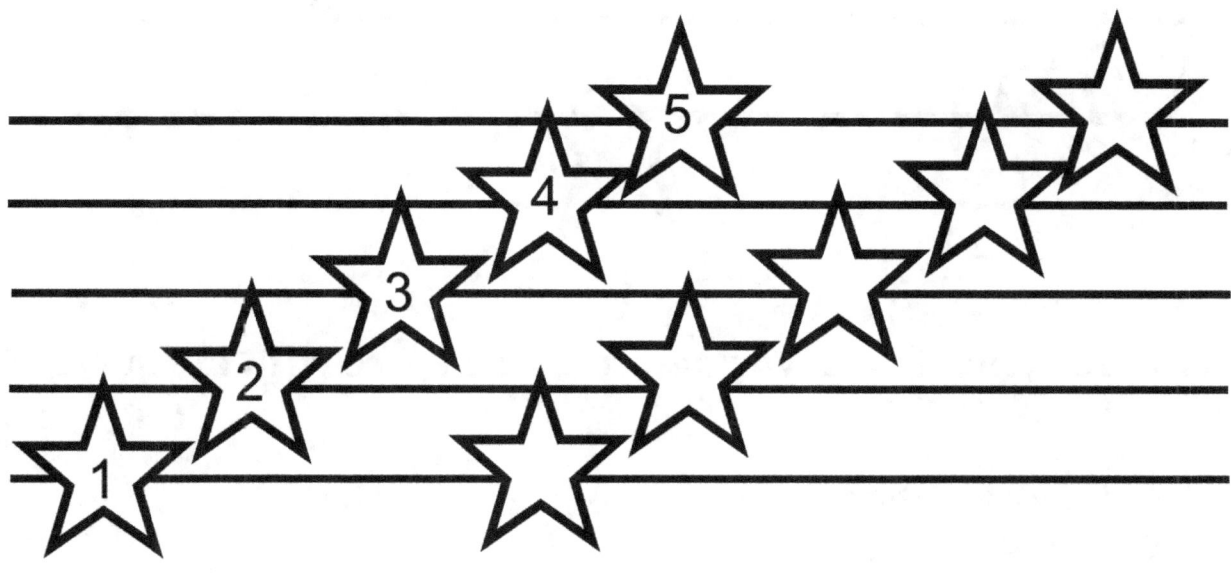

2. Use a colored pencil or crayon and trace the correct line with the matching color.

- ❖ Line 1 - Blue
- ❖ Line 2 - Red
- ❖ Line 3 - Purple
- ❖ Line 4 - Orange
- ❖ Line 5 - Green

Like the line numbers, we count the spaces starting at the lowest space.

3. Write the space numbers in each star starting at the bottom space.

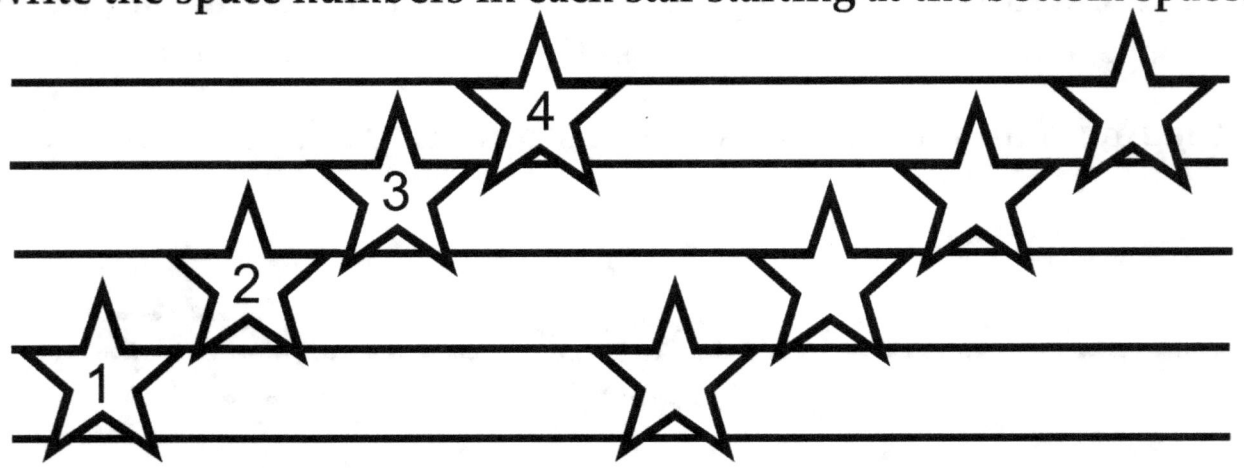

4. Use a colored pencil or crayon and color the space with the matching color.

- ❖ Space 1 – Blue
- ❖ Space 2 – Red
- ❖ Space 3 – Purple
- ❖ Space 4 – Orange

5. Write the beats in the hearts and the counts on the lines.

The Magic of Music Theory Pre-Reading B - © 2024 Horsehair Music. Photocopying prohibited.

Lesson 25

1. Write the space numbers in the triangles and line numbers in the hexagons beginning at the bottom.

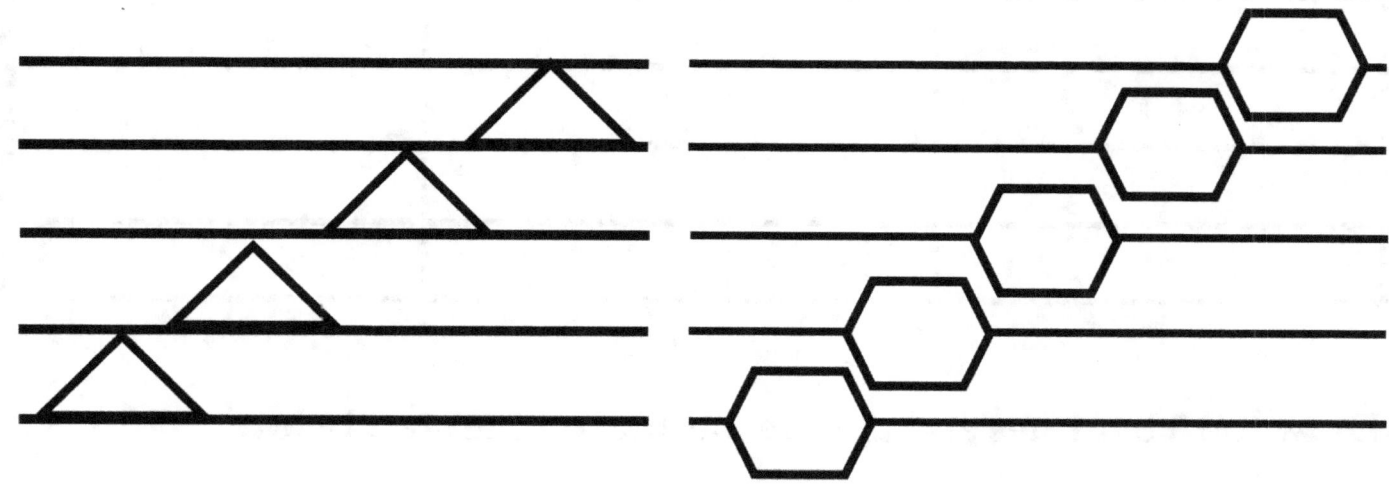

2. Trace the whole notes stepping up on the staff. Color the line notes orange and the space notes green.

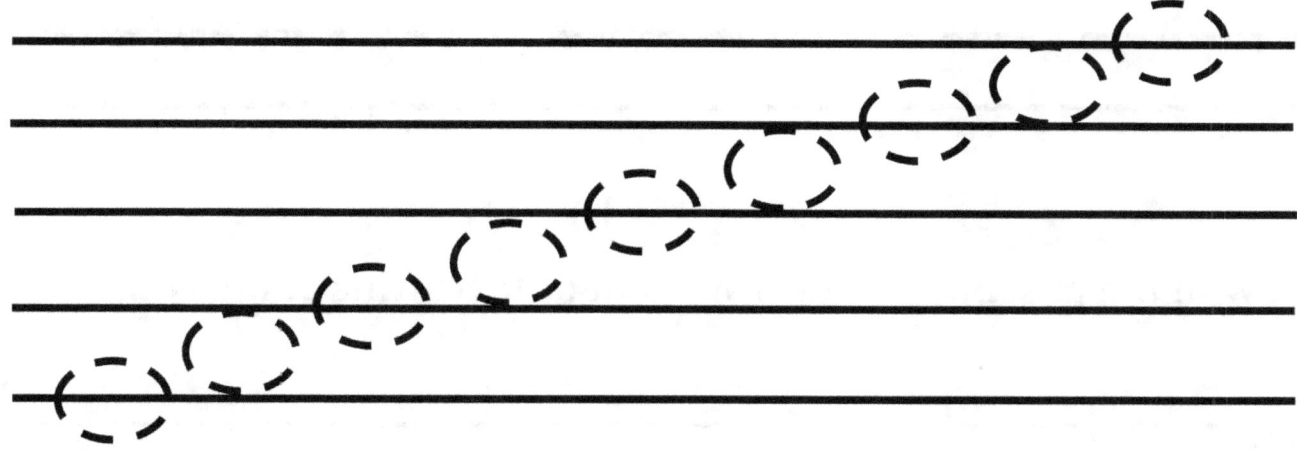

3. How many line notes are orange? _____

4. How many space notes are green? _____

5. How many notes are on the staff? _____

To draw bar lines and double bar lines on the staff, the bar line touches line 1 and line 5. *Do not let the bar line cross line 1 or line 5.*

6. Trace the bar lines and double bar line.

7. Draw the 3 bar lines and double bar line on the staff below.

8. Draw in the missing bar lines and a double bar line at the end.

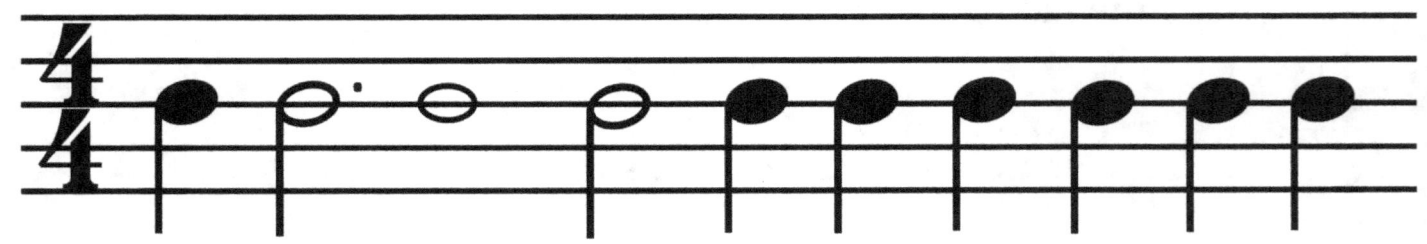

Lesson 26

1. Put your pencil on the lowest dot and count up to the line or space number. Draw a whole note on the correct line or space.

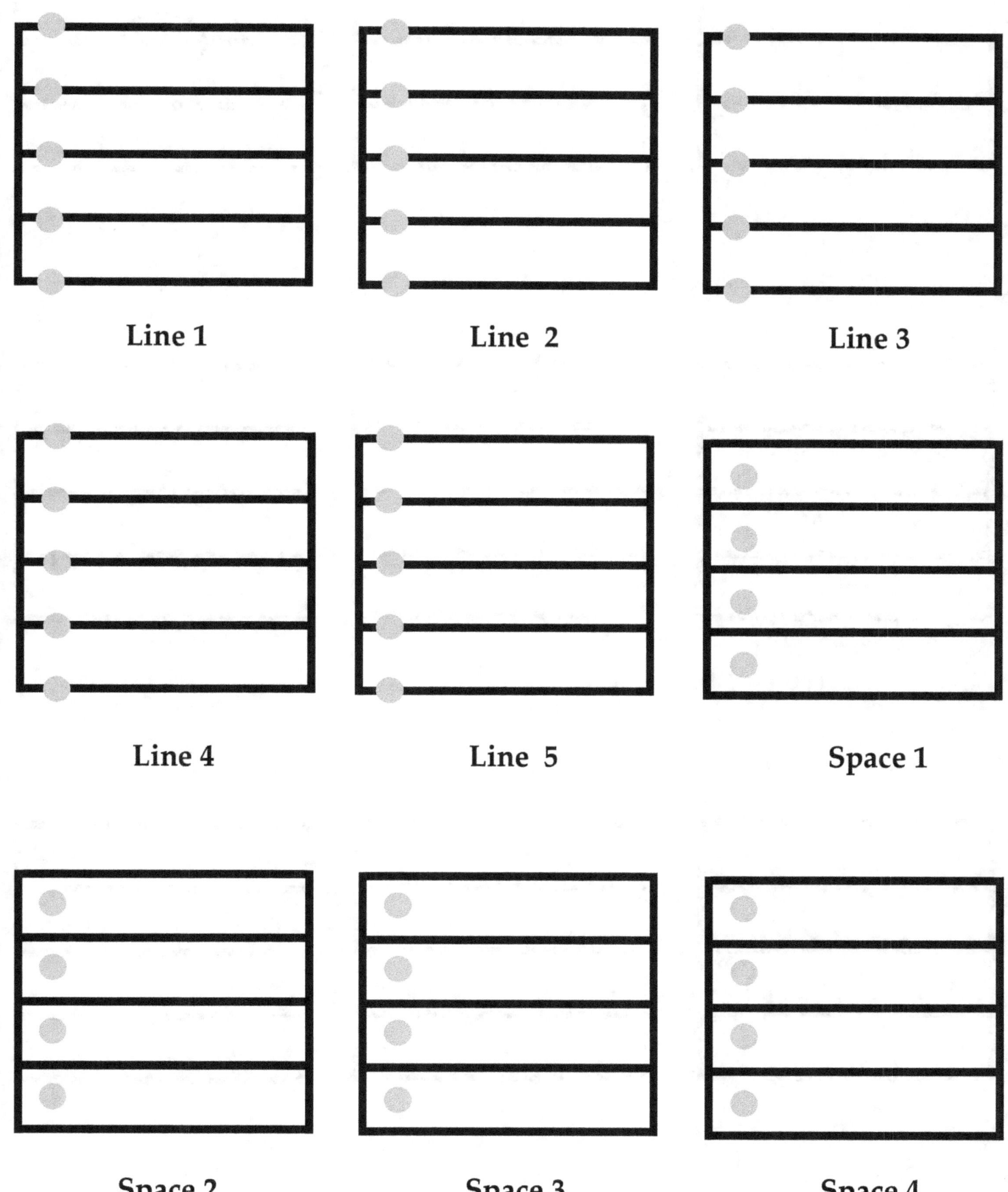

Line 1   Line 2   Line 3

Line 4   Line 5   Space 1

Space 2   Space 3   Space 4

2. Write the line or space number for each note.

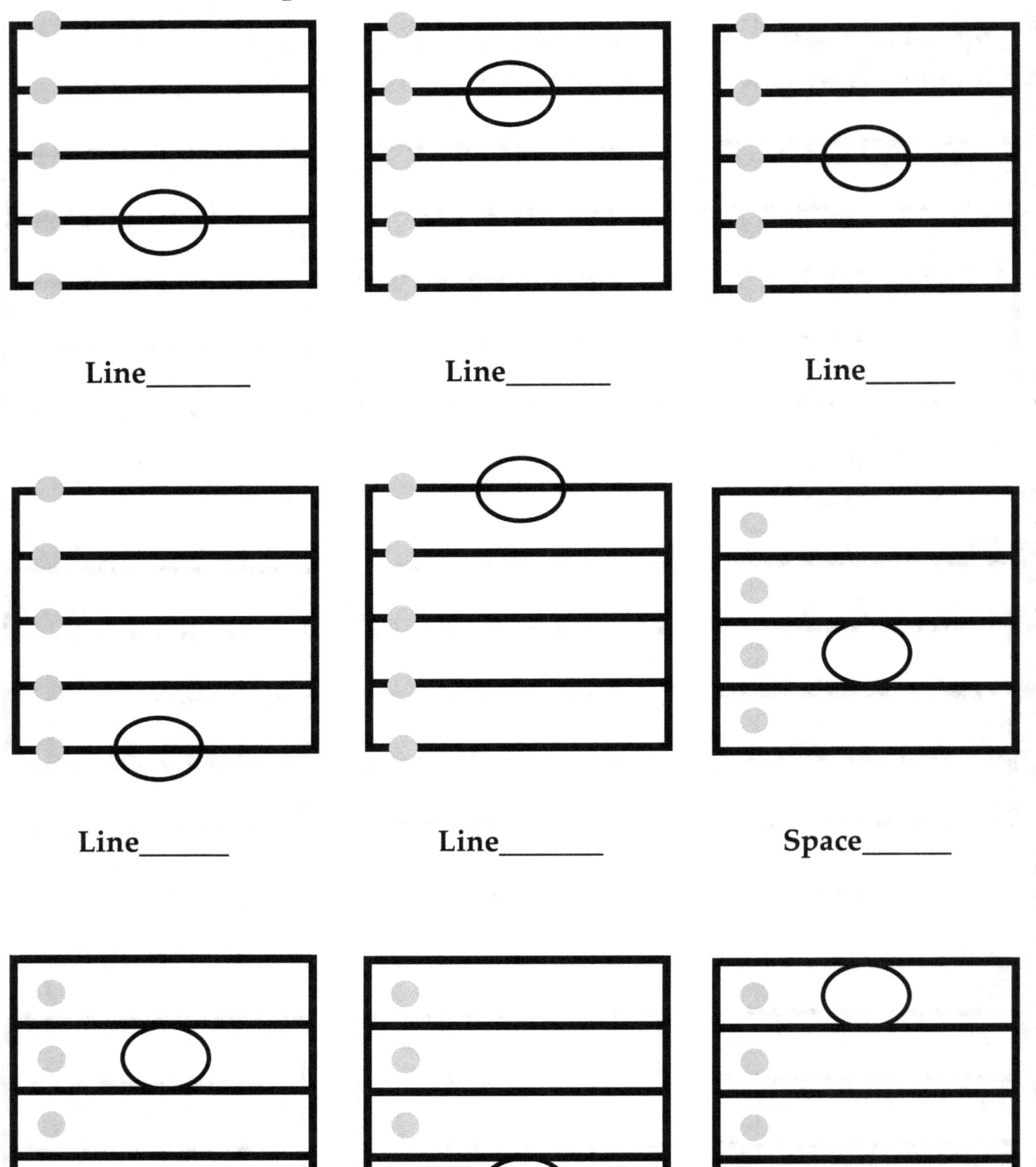

Line_____

Line_____

Line_____

Line_____

Line_____

Space_____

Space_____

Space_____

Space_____

Lesson 27

1. Write the letters in the empty houses. Circle if the notes go up or down.

UP   DOWN   SAME   UP   DOWN   SAME   UP   DOWN   SAME

2. Write the top number for the time signature.

3. Draw a whole note on the correct line.

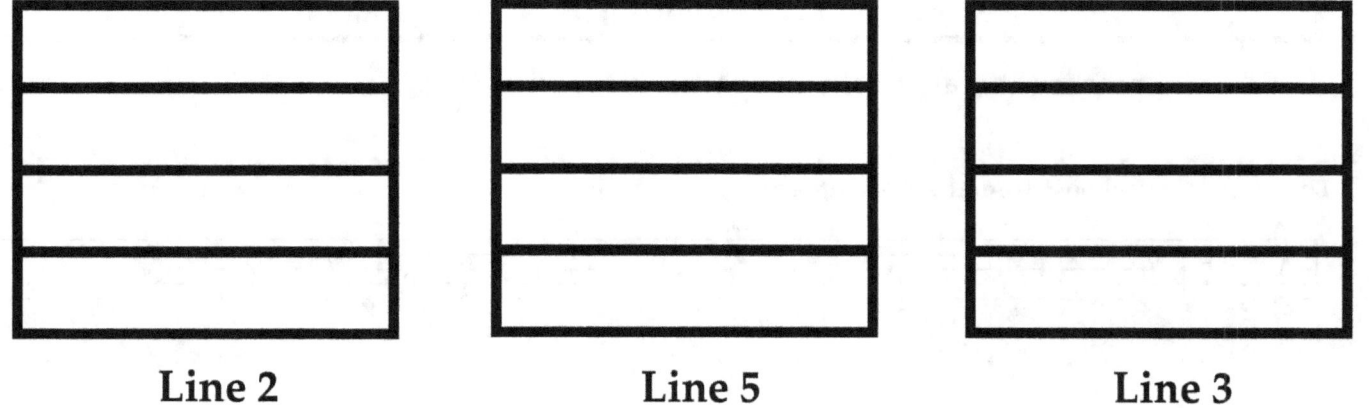

Line 2   Line 5   Line 3

What do you hear? #6

You will hear several notes for each box. When you hear a long note, draw a line. When you hear a short note, draw a dot. Draw all the notes that you hear in the order that you hear them.

Long Note = ━━━━━ **Short Note =** ●

```
┌─────────────────────┐   ┌─────────────────────┐
│ 1.                  │   │ 2.                  │
│                     │   │                     │
│                     │   │                     │
│                     │   │                     │
│                     │   │                     │
│                     │   │                     │
│                     │   │                     │
└─────────────────────┘   └─────────────────────┘
┌─────────────────────┐   ┌─────────────────────┐
│ 3.                  │   │ 4.                  │
│                     │   │                     │
│                     │   │                     │
│                     │   │                     │
│                     │   │                     │
│                     │   │                     │
│                     │   │                     │
└─────────────────────┘   └─────────────────────┘
```

* For extra practice at drawing rhythm patterns, see page 81.

The teacher may choose from these examples:

Lesson 28

The Three Clefs

nce upon a time, three bears lived in a house in the big woods. There was a Papa Bear, a Mama Bear, and a Baby Bear. The three bears had visited Goldie's Music Store and found instruments that were just right for them. Papa Bear chose the cello. He liked the low sounds of the cello. Mama Bear was learning to play the viola. She Liked the mellow and soothing sounds the viola made. The viola didn't play low notes like the cello, and it didn't play the high notes like the violin. The viola notes were right in the middle. Baby Bear picked the violin. It was the smallest of the string family. And the violin could make high sounds like he did when his dad tickled him. But Baby Bear had found that he could growl on the G string and sound a little bit like Papa Bear.

One morning at breakfast, Papa Bear said, "I think we should go to Goldie's Music Store today to get some music books." Mama Bear agreed and said, "Let's lock our door this time, so we don't have any little girls trying our porridge, chairs, and beds! That gave me quite a fright last time we got home from Goldie's." "Good idea!" said Papa Bear. "I'll go look for my keys. Baby Bear, are you ready to go?"

Soon the three bears were on their way to Goldie's Music store. They saw My Strow as they walked in the door. "Hello, My Strow," said Papa Bear. "It's good to see you again! Could you help us find some music books?" "I would love to help you," said My Strow.

My Strow picked up a sticky note and said, "Let's start with Baby Bear first. He will need music in the treble clef." My Strow drew a swirling symbol on the sticky note. "This is called the treble clef. Treble means high. Because the violin plays high notes, violinist read music that is written in using the treble clef." The three bears and My Strow walked over to the violin music bin. My Strow picked up a book that said, *The Little Bear's Guide to Violin.* "Here we go, this one will be perfect for you." "This looks fun!" said Baby Bear. "I can't wait to go home and practice. Thank you My Strow!"

"Now let's look over here in the viola music bin for some music for Mama Bear?" said My Strow. "Mama Bear will need a book that uses the alto clef. Did you know that only violists read music in the alto clef? And sometimes it is called the viola clef!" said My Strow. "Oh my!" said Mama Bear. "How very special! What does an alto clef look like My Strow?"

My Strow pulled off another sticky note from his pad and drew an alto clef. "Some people call it the C clef because it points to where C is on the music staff." My Strow rummaged in the bin and finally pulled out a book. "Ah, here is the book! *Hibernation Tunes in Alto Clef.* My Strow opened the book and held it for Mama Bear to see. "See how each line has an alto clef?" Mama Bear nodded and said, "Thank you. My Strow, I think this book will be great!"

My Strow looked at Papa Bear and said, "Now, Papa Bear, your cello music will be over here. Cellists read music in the bass clef. We say "base" clef, like baseball. It's not bass like the fish!" My Strow pulled off another sticky note and drew the bass clef. "The bass clef looks like half of a heart with 3 dots! Bass means low. Since the cello plays low notes, they read music in the bass clef." "I learned something new today!" said Papa Bear. "Does every instrument have their own clef?" "No," said My Strow. "Other instruments read music using the treble and bass clef. In fact, pianists have to read music in both treble clef and bass clef at the same time!" "Whew! I'm glad I only have one clef to read." said Papa Bear.

The three bears paid for their books. "Thank you, My Strow. It is always good to see you and you are so helpful!" My Strow smiled and said, "I'm always happy to help the three bears! I am the conductor for the orchestra, and we have a concert this weekend. We are playing a piece that is supposed to sound like animals. It's called *Carnival of the Animals* by Camile Saint-Saens. We are also playing a piece called *Bear Dance* by Bela Bartok. I know you would like that one!" "We will go right home and order our tickets. Thanks for telling us, My Strow!" said Papa Bear. My Strow smiled and said, "You will be able to see me since stand right in the middle waving a baton." My Strow waved to the three bears as they headed back to their house in the woods with the books tucked safely under their arms!

THE END

1. Listen to a recording of Partita No 3 in E Major by Johann Sebastian Bach. Color the treble clef and listen to the violin's high, treble clef notes.

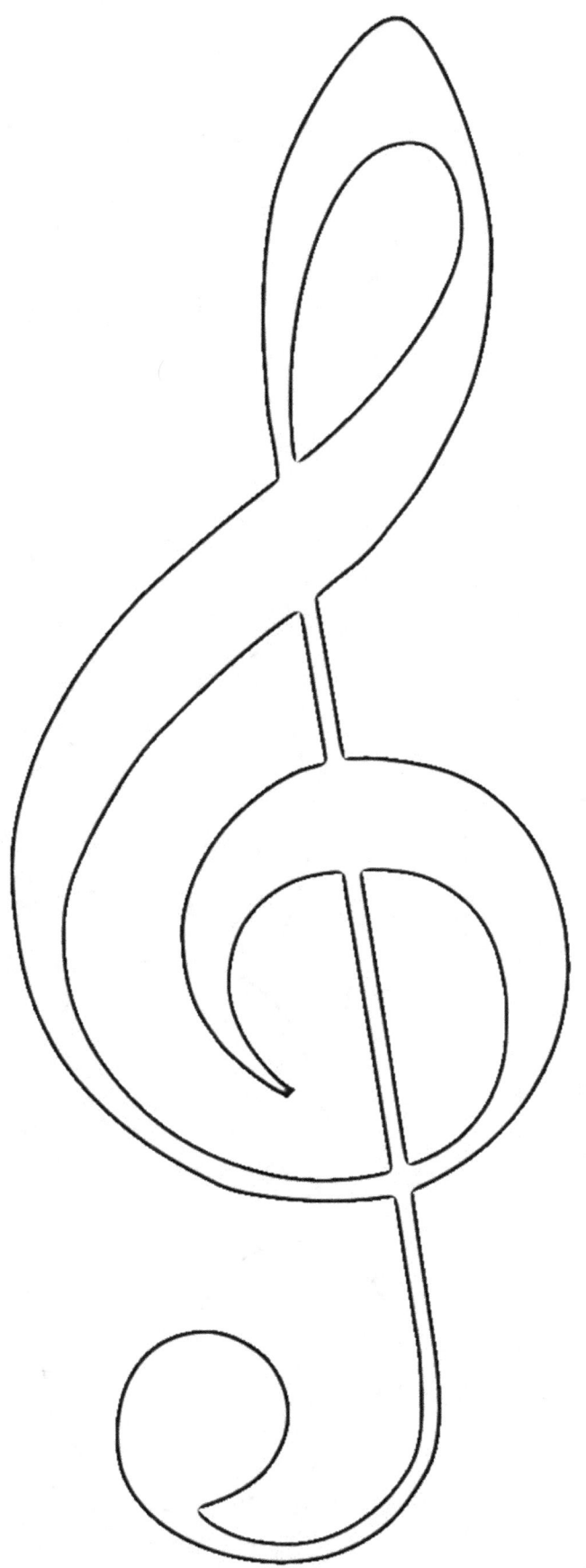

2. Listen to a recording of Bach's Suite No. 3 in C Major, V. Boureé, played by a viola. Color the alto clef while you listen to the viola's middle notes.

3. Listen to a recording of Cello Suite No. 1 in G Major, I. Prelude, by Johann Sebastian Bach. Color the bass clef while you listen to the cello's low notes!

Lesson 29

How to draw a treble clef.

Step 1	Step 2	Step 3	Step 4	Step 5
Draw a tall J. Start above the staff.	Draw a big D. Start at the top of the J touch line 4.	Draw a big C. Start at line 4 touch line 1.	Draw a big D. Start at line 1 touch line 3.	Draw a little c. Start at line 3 curl around line 2.

1. Trace the treble clefs.

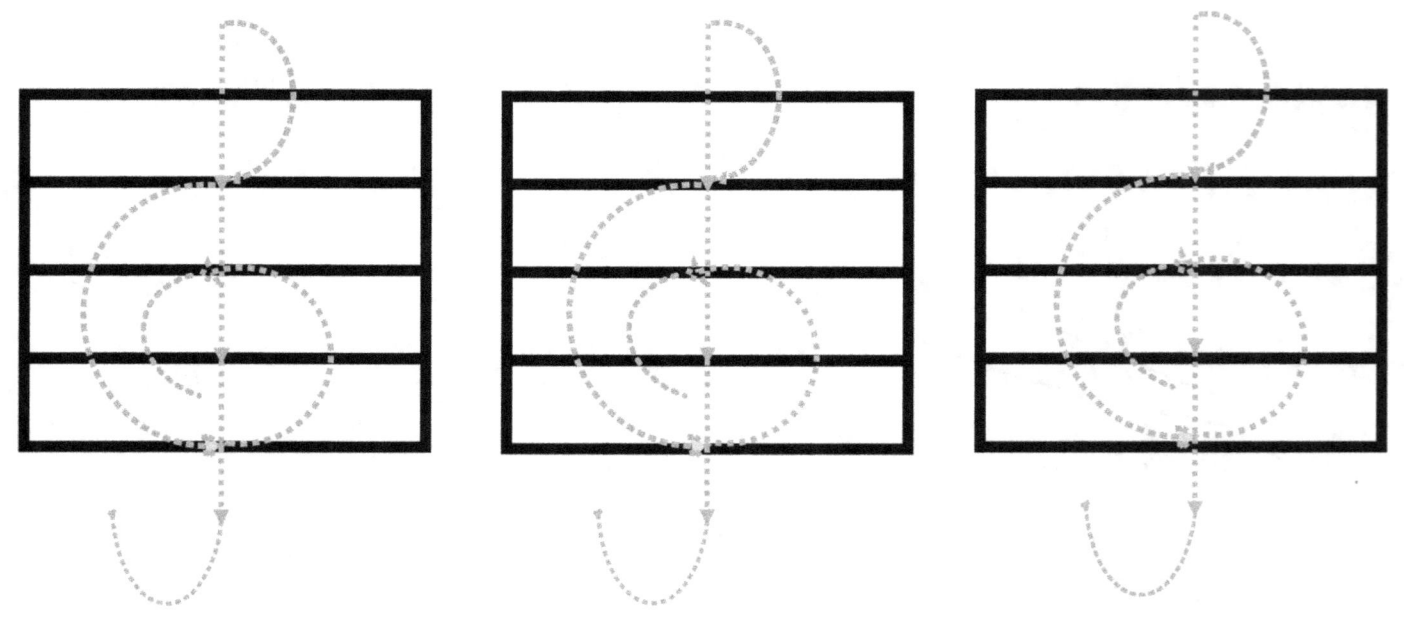

Step 1	Step 2	Step 3	Step 4	Step 5
Tall J. Start above the staff.	Big D. Start at the top of the J touch line 4.	Big C. Start at line 4 touch line 1.	Big D. Start at line 1 touch line 3.	Little c. Start at line 3 curl around line 2.

2. Trace the treble clef. Then try drawing one on your own.

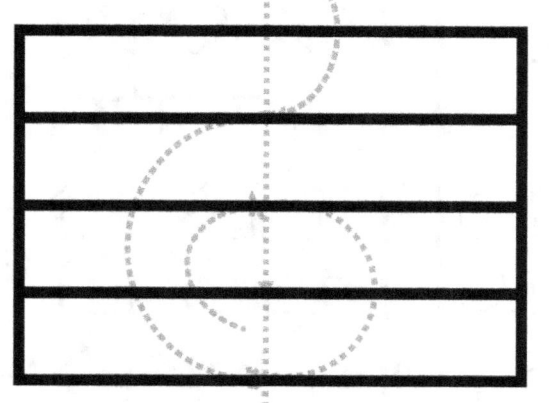

3. Circle the correct answer.

A. Treble means: low   high   you have been bad

B. What clef do violins use?   Alto Clef   Bass Clef   Treble Clef

C. What clef to cellos use?   Alto Clef   Bass Clef   Treble Clef

D. What clef to violas use?   Alto Clef   Bass Clef   Treble Clef

E. Bass means: low   high   a kind of fish

F. A composer: flies airplanes   writes music   makes compost

G. How many players are in a string quartet?   1   2   3   4

Lesson 30

1. Color the house that matches the letter at the end of each string.

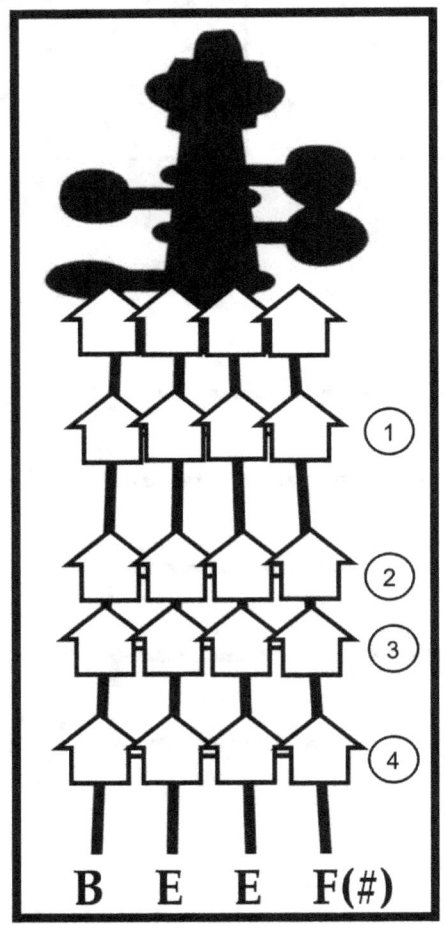

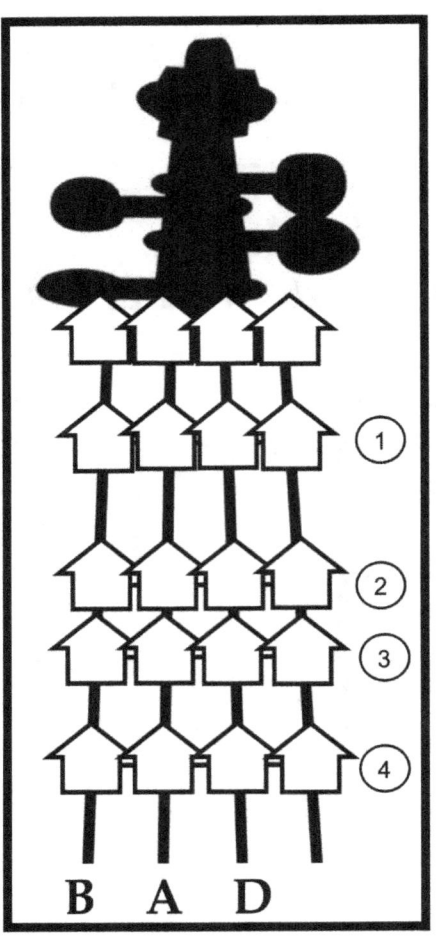

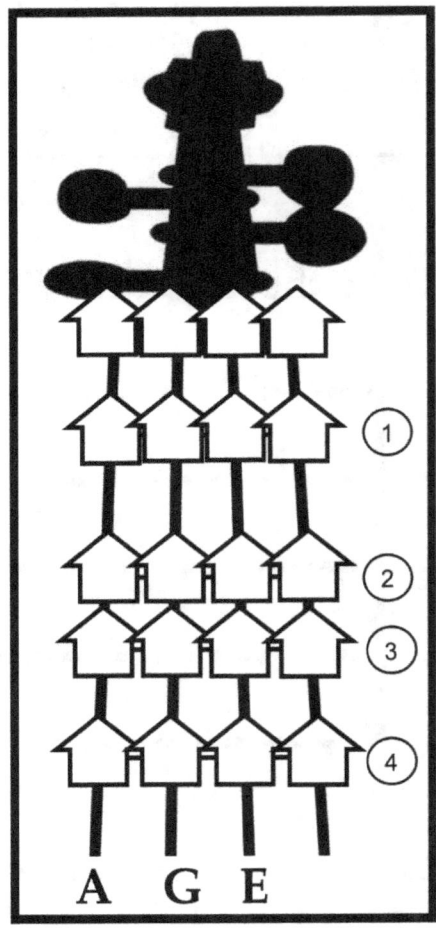

2. Write the top number for the time signature in the box.

3. Circle if the note is a line note or space note.

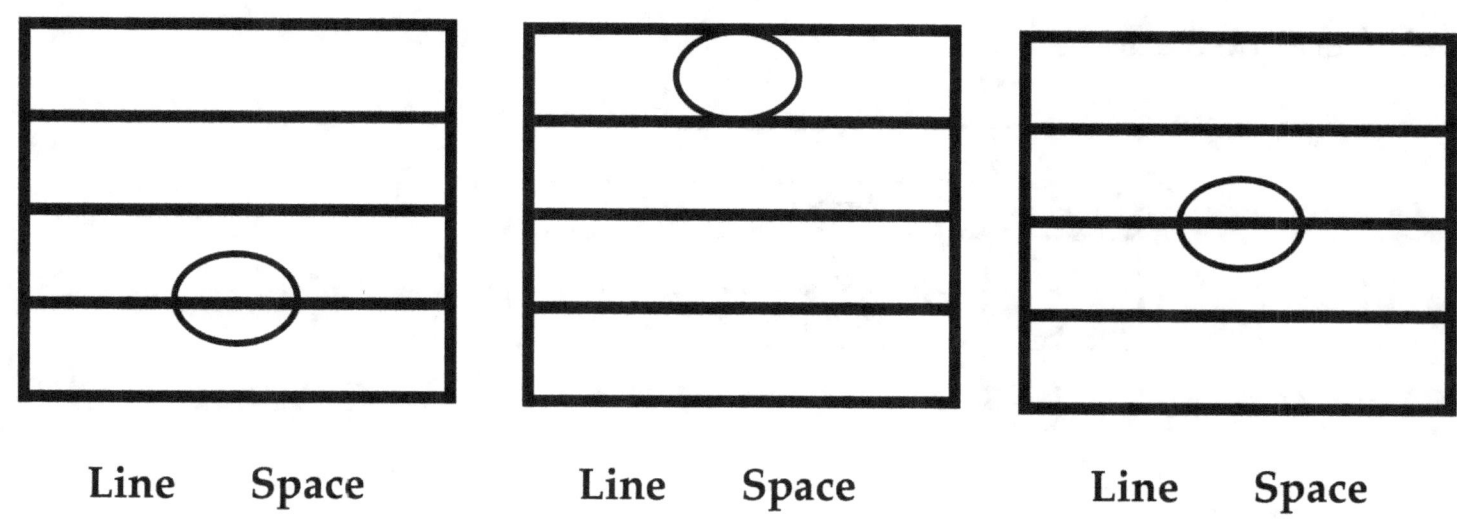

Line   Space   Line   Space   Line   Space

4. Write the line number or space number in the blank. Remember to count up from the bottom line or space.

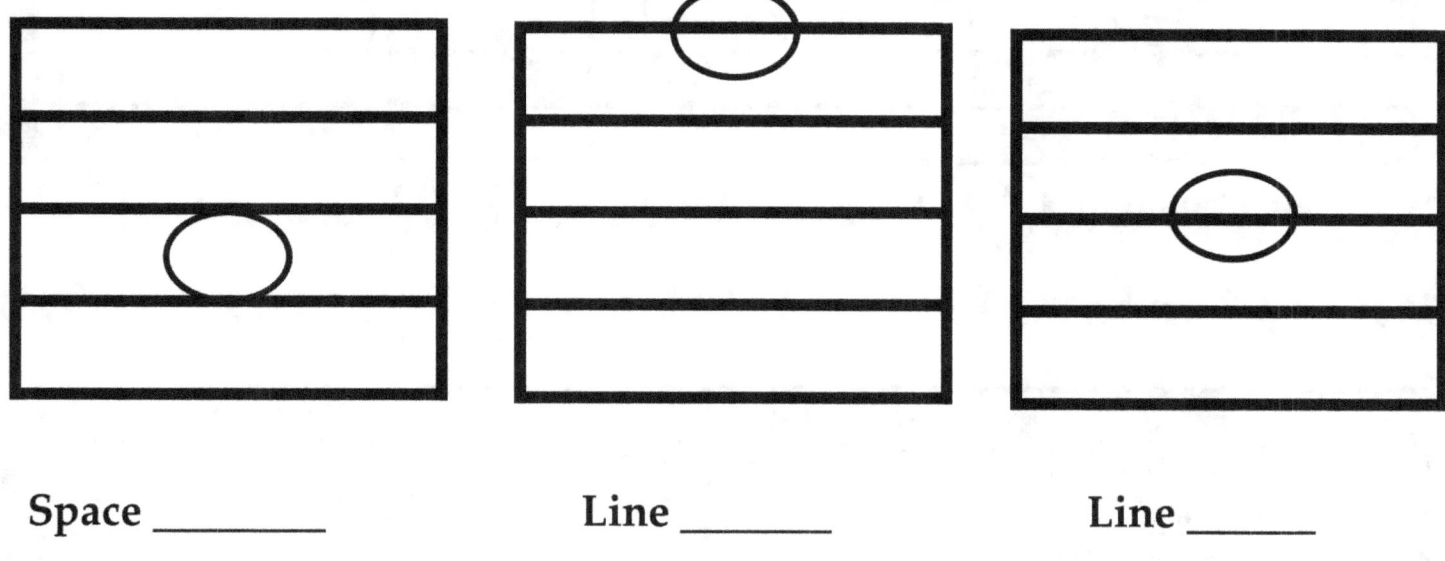

Space _____   Line _____   Line _____

5. Draw the missing bar lines and double bar lines.

The time signature goes on the staff on the right side of the clef. The bottom number is written between line 1 and 3. The top number is written between line 3 and 5.

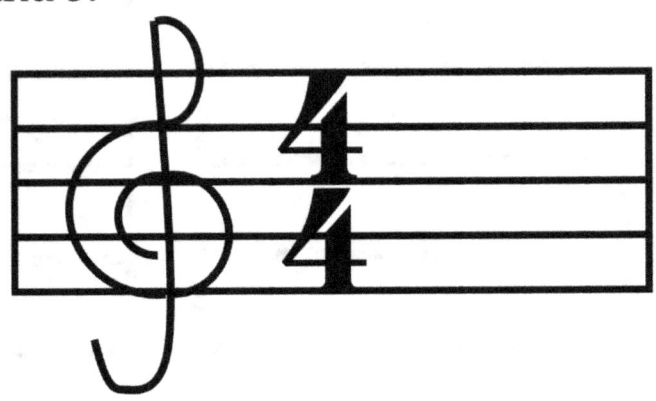

6. Write the beats for each note in the heart and the counts on the lines.

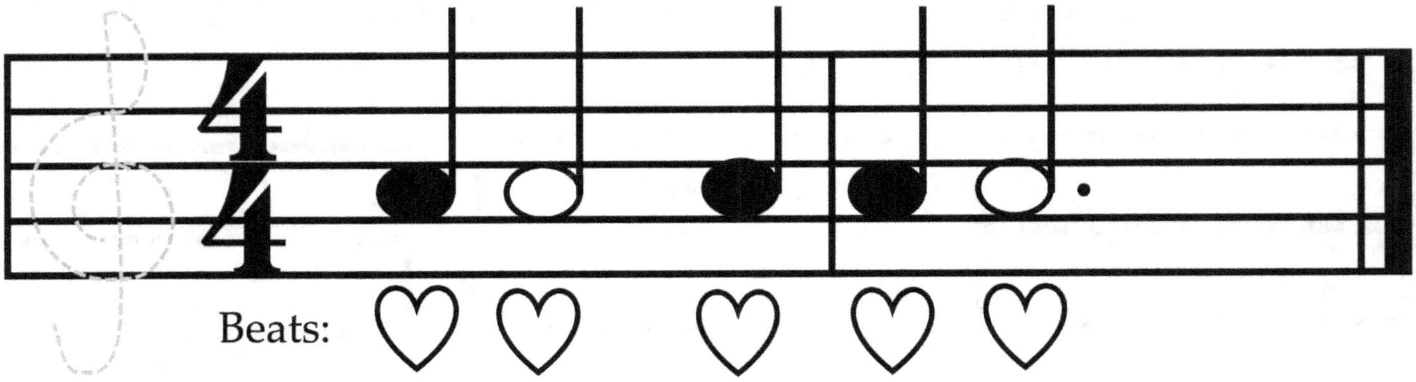

Beats:

Counts: _ _ _ _ _ _ _ _ _ _

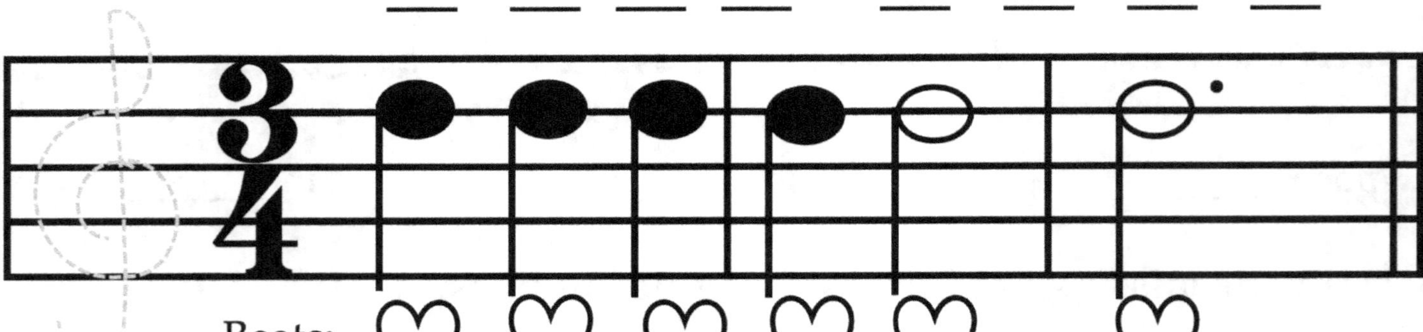

Beats:

Counts: _ _ _ _ _ _

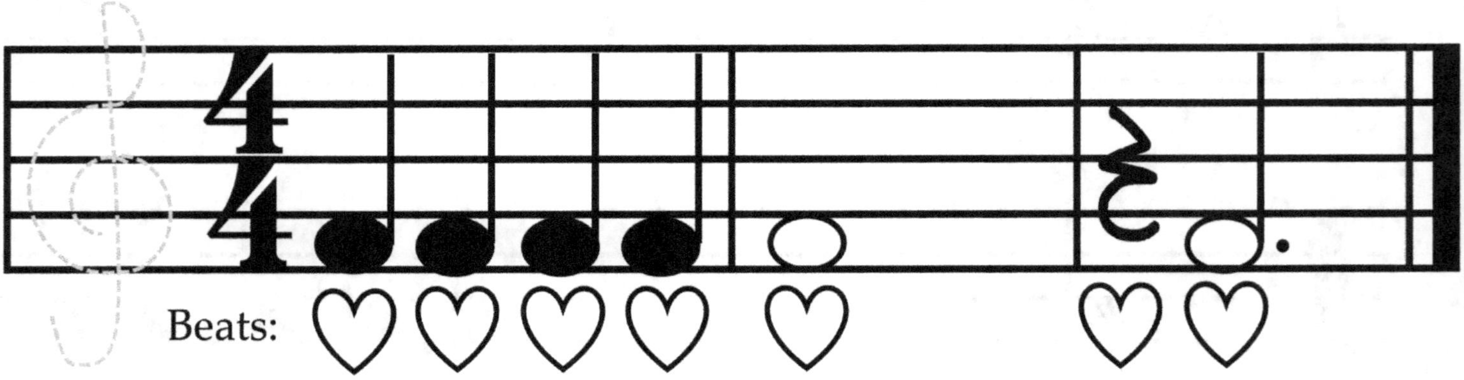

Beats:

Counts: _ _ _ _ _ _

Glossary

Alto Clef – Violas read music using the alto clef. Sometimes called the C clef because the clef points to C line on the staff.

Bar Line – A vertical line through the staff touching line 1 and 5. Creates measures.

Bass Clef – Cellos read music using the bass clef. Sometimes called the F clef because the clef points to F line on the staff.

Composer – A person who writes or composes music.

Dotted Half Note – Gets 3 beats in 4/4 time.

Double Bar Line – A thin line followed by a thick line. Signals the end the piece.

Dynamics – Markings and terms that show what volume to play.

Forte – [dynamic] Italian word meaning loud.

Half Note – Gets 2 beats in 4/4 time.

Half Rest – Silence for 2 beats in 4/4 time.

Interval – The distance between two notes. Must include the first pitch when counting.

Measures – Space between bar lines. Organizes the notes into groups.

Mezzo Forte – [dynamic] Italian word meaning medium loud.

Music Alphabet – First seven letters of the English alphabet.

Piano – [dynamic] Italian word meaning soft.

Quarter Note – Gets 1 beat in 4/4 time.

Quarter Rest – Silence for 1 beat in 4/4 time.

Rhythm – The organizations of notes into groups.

Staff – 5 lines and 4 spaces that show pitches.

String Quartet – 4 players; 2 violins, 1 viola, 1 cello.

Time Signature – The top number tells how many beats are in each measure. The bottom number tells what kind of note gets 1 beat. A 4 on the bottom means the quarter note gets 1 beat.

Treble Clef – Treble means high. Violins read music using the treble clef. Sometimes called the G clef because the clef points to G line on the staff.

Whole Note – Gets 4 beats in 4/4 time.

Whole Rest – Silence for 4 beats in 4/4 time, or rest for a whole measure.

Extra Ear Training Practice A
Up or Down

If the notes you hear step up, color the up arrow. If the notes you hear step down, color the down arrow.

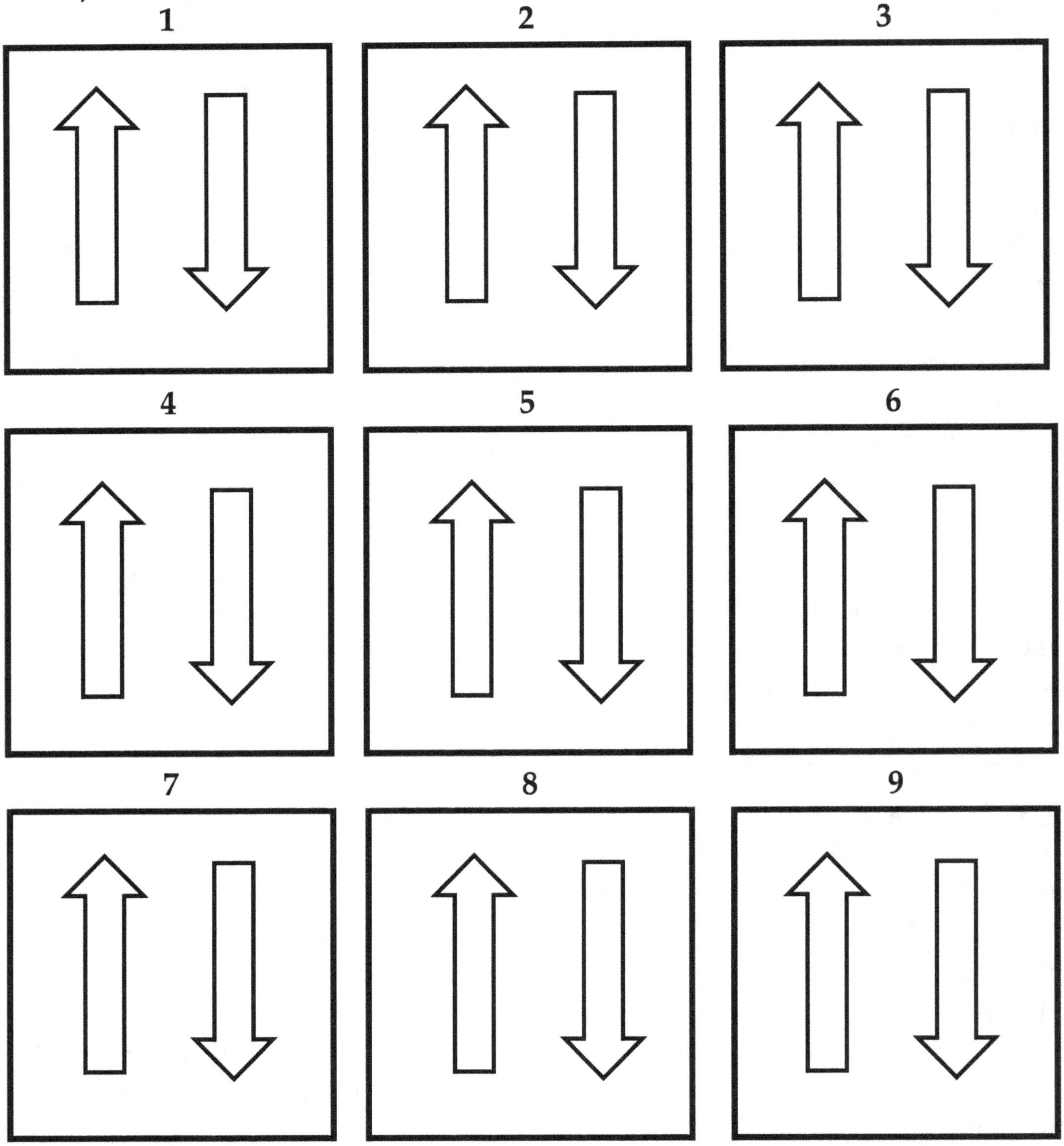

1

2

3

4

5

6

7

8

9

The teacher may choose from these examples:

Extra Ear Training Practice B
Dynamics

Circle the dynamic you hear.

1

f

mf

p

2

f

mf

p

3

f

mf

p

4

f

mf

p

5

f

mf

p

6

f

mf

p

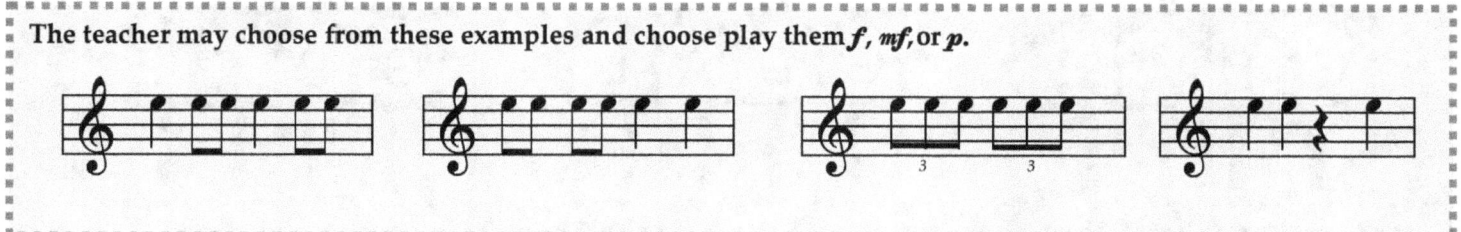

The teacher may choose from these examples and choose play them f, mf, or p.

Extra Ear Training Practice C
Identify Open Strings

Color the house of the string that you hear.

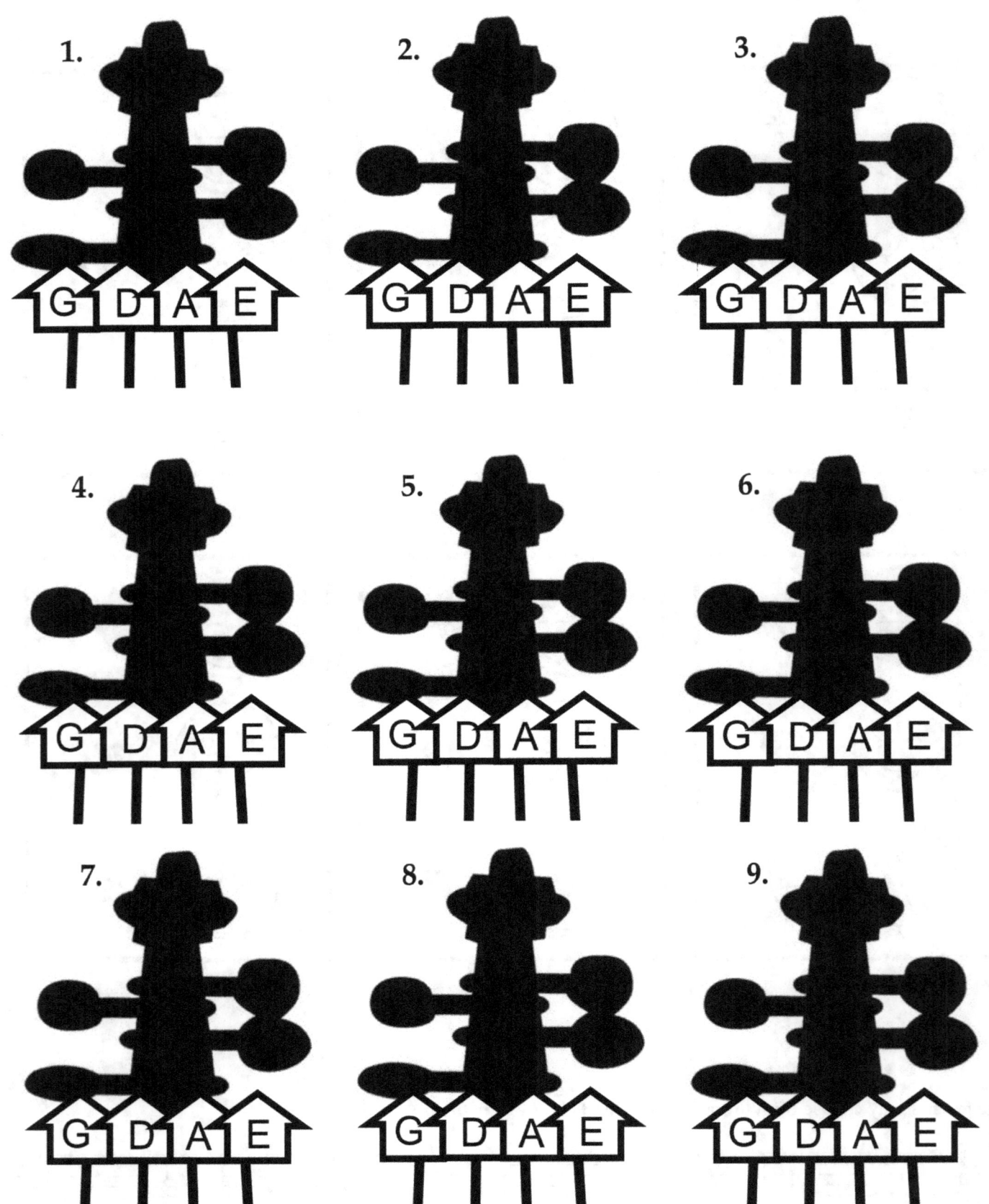

Extra Ear Training Practice D
Long and Short Patterns

You will hear several notes for each box. When you hear a long note, draw a line. When you hear a short note, draw a dot. Draw all of the notes that you hear in the order that you hear them.

1.

2.

3.

4.

The teacher may choose from these examples:

Hooray!

_____

has completed

The Magic of Music Theory
Pre-Reading B

and is now ready for Primer

_____

(Teacher)

_____

(Date)

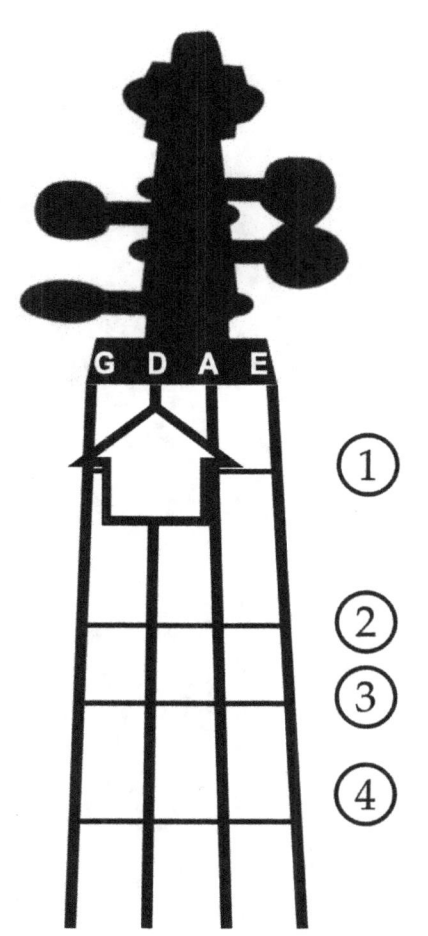

① ② ③ ④

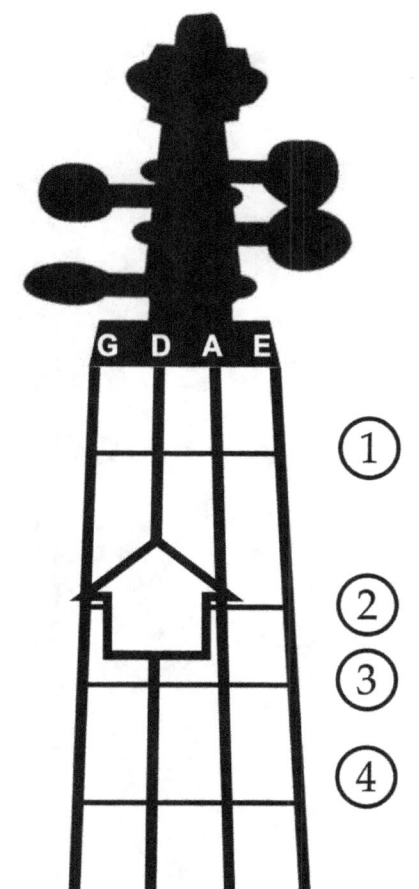

① ② ③ ④

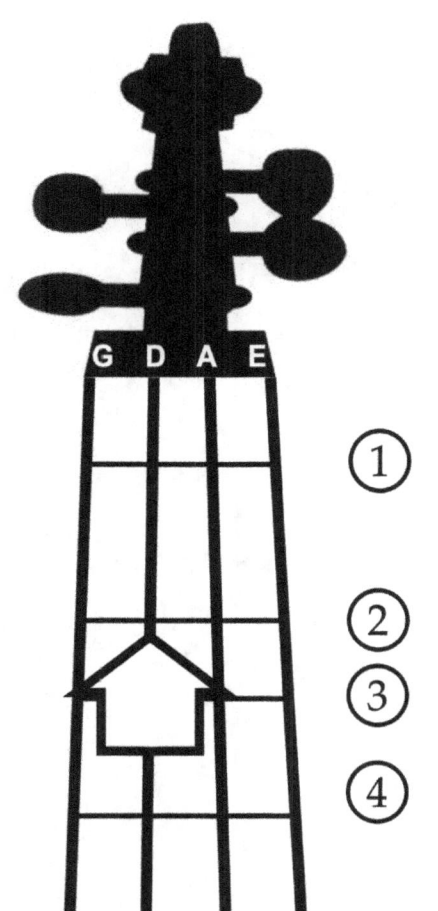

① ② ③ ④

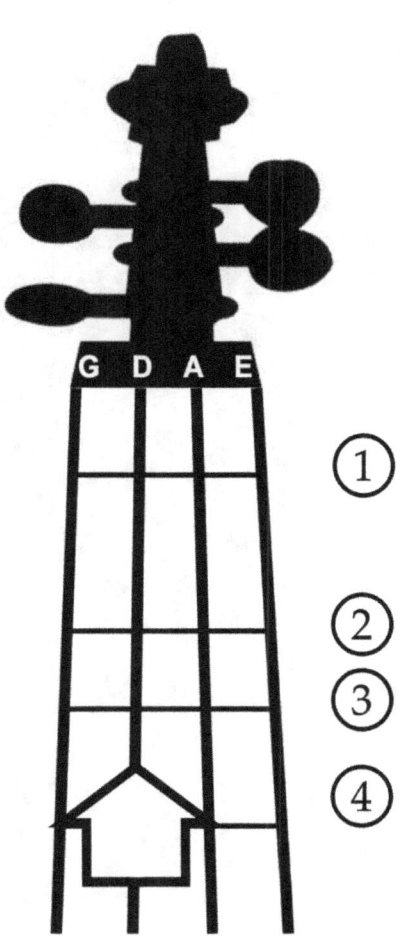

① ② ③ ④

F#

E

G

A

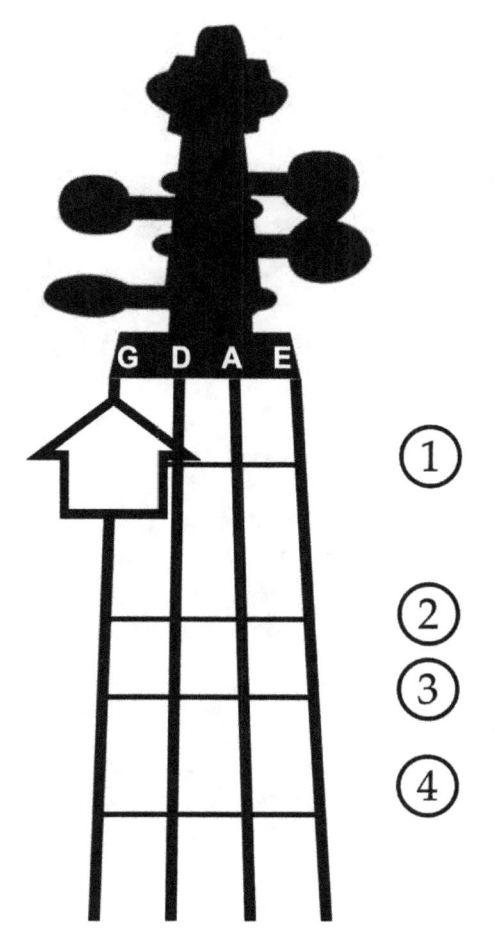

①

②
③
④

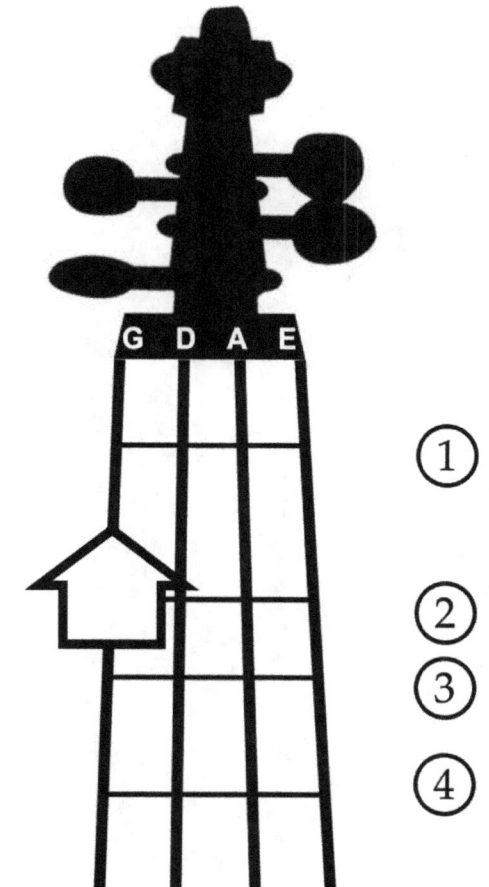

①

②
③
④

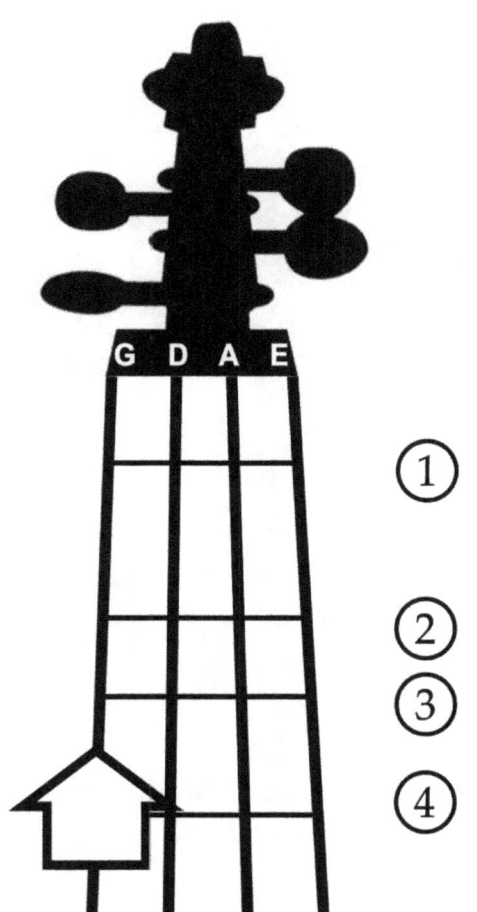

①

②
③

④

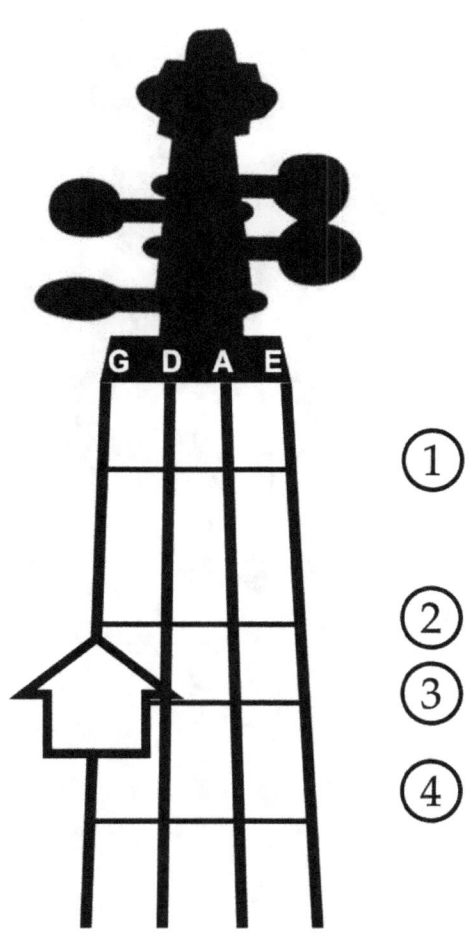

①

②
③

④

B

A

D

C

ξ

4
4

Half Rest

2 Beats

Quarter Rest

1 Beat

Whole Rest

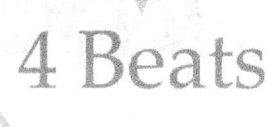

4 Beats

Time Signature

4 Beats in every measure.

A 4 on the bottom means the quarter note gets 1 beat.

Alto Clef

Treble Clef

Treble = High

Bass Clef

Bass = Low

Time Signature

3 Beats in every measure.

A 4 on the bottom means the quarter note gets 1 beat.